Circular ⊔⊓⊓kS

in

East Devon

Simone Stanbrook-Byrne
and
James Clancy

CULM VALLEY PUBLISHING

Published by

Culm Valley Publishing Ltd
Farmers
3 Ashley Road, Uffculme
Cullompton, Devon
EX15 3AH, UK
Tel: +44(0)1884 840172 Fax: +44(0)1884 840515
E-mail: info@culmvalleypublishing.co.uk
Website: www.culmvalleypublishing.co.uk

First published 2013, reprinted with revisions 2015

ISBN 978-1-907942-08-2 paperback

British Library Cataloguing-in-Publication Data
A catalogue record for this book is available from the British Library

Typeset by Culm Valley Publishing Ltd
Printed and bound by Ashford Colour Press Ltd, Gosport, Hampshire

Front cover image: Ladram Bay (Walk 10)
Back cover image: Fire Beacon Plantation (Walk 15)
All images used in this book are available as cards and prints from Culm Valley Publishing

Contents

Introduction

Writing this walking guide has been an enjoyable undertaking: fabulous views, route-finding on elusive paths, country inns with open fires or sunny gardens – and the reward of ending the day back where we started. Some of the walks within this guide are very short but are close together so you could easily do two in the same day's walking.

On any walk common sense must prevail: be properly shod and take care where you put your feet, be prepared for any kind of weather, take food and first aid supplies with you and make sure someone knows where you're going. Mobile phones are often useless in the middle of nowhere.

We feel it's important that you take the **correct OS map** with you plus a **compass**, and are conversant with their use. Our sketch maps are precisely that – sketches – and are for rough guidance only and not necessarily to scale.

You know you've had a good day's walking when you get home safely at the end of it.

Follow the countryside code:
www.naturalengland.org.uk/ourwork/enjoying/countrysidecode/default.aspx

Our grateful thanks to:

Els Damen and Peter Scholten for 'international input' on the Otterton walk.
Margaret Davidson and Sue Jackson, Simone's back-up team on the Tipton St. John walk.
Dan Hargreaves for historical information on the Sidbury walk.
Nic, Ella and William Clancy & Tony Byrne for being dragged along so often.

Disclaimer

Points that should be borne in mind on any route:

Public footpaths can be legally re-routed from the path shown on the map. In such cases they are usually clearly signposted. Where this has happened before the time of writing it has been noted in the text.

Most public footpaths are on private land. Please respect this.

Don't be surprised to find livestock grazing on public footpaths – and treat all animals with caution and respect.

If a field is planted with crops across a footpath, provision is usually made around the edge of the field.

Landmarks can change: trees and hedges may disappear; streams can dry up in warm weather or flood after heavy rain; stiles turn into gates and vice versa; fences appear where previously there was no boundary. Even views are different as the seasons progress. In such cases a modicum of common sense must be exercised – in conjunction with the OS map.

Public footpaths are at times blocked by barbed wire etc. Should this render the route impassable find the shortest detour around that section.

Please leave gates as you find them and if you have to climb them do so at the hinge end where it's stronger.

Exercise caution on wet stiles – they can be extremely slippery.

Take all your rubbish with you, please don't damage anything during the walk and please don't pick plants.

Please keep your dogs under proper control.

We hope that you enjoy these walks without mishap, but urge you to exercise common sense at all times. Neither the authors nor Culm Valley Publishing Ltd accepts responsibility for any misadventure that may occur during, or arise from, these walks and suggested routes.

Walk Locations

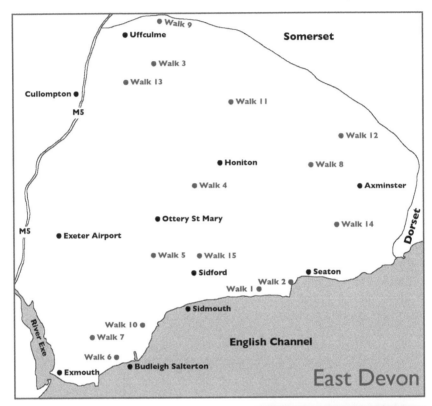

Walk 9
● Uffculme
Somerset
● Walk 3
● Walk 13
Cullompton ●
M5
● Walk 11
● Walk 12
● Walk 8
● Honiton
● Walk 4
● Axminster
● Ottery St Mary
M5
● Walk 14
● Exeter Airport
Dorset
● Walk 5   ● Walk 15
● Sidford   ● Seaton
Walk 2 ●
Walk 1 ●
● Sidmouth
River Exe
Walk 10 ●
● Walk 7
English Channel
Walk 6 ●
● Exmouth   ● Budleigh Salterton
East Devon

Open the gate please! (Walk 9)

Walk 1
Branscombe
Distance: 4¼ miles / 6.8km

This lovely walk starts in one of Devon's most picturesque villages and encompasses a fabulous section of the Jurassic Coast (see feature on Otterton walk). It can be rather rough underfoot in places and involves some ascents and descents but these are more than made up for by the glorious scenery and prevalence of good refreshment stops. Dolphins are sighted from time to time off the coast here so you may be lucky enough to see them.

Map: OS Explorer 115, Exmouth & Sidmouth and OS Explorer 116, Lyme Regis & Bridport

Start point: Branscombe Village Hall. Post code: EX12 3DB. Grid ref: SY197887

Directions to start: Branscombe is on the coast of East Devon, signed off the A3052 east of Sidmouth

Parking: Branscombe Village Hall Car Park. Post code: EX12 3DB

Public Transport: Bus 899 operated by Axe Valley Mini-Travel passes through Branscombe. Timetables available online at www.travelinesw.com. Nearest railway station is Honiton (7.6 miles)

Distance: 4¼ miles

Refreshments: Fountain Head Inn, Street, Nr. Branscombe, 01297 680359; Masons Arms, Branscombe, 01297 680300; Old Bakery Tea Rooms, Branscombe, 01297 680333; Sea Shanty, Branscombe Mouth, 01297 680577. All the aforementioned should be contacted to confirm opening times as they vary throughout the year

Toilets: Behind Branscombe Village Hall and at Branscombe Mouth

Nearby places to stay: The Bulstone, 01297 680446; Great Seaside, 01297 680470; The Masons Arms, Branscombe, 01297 680300

Nearby places of interest: Beer Quarry Caves, 01297 680282; Branscombe Forge (NT), 01297 680333/680481; The Donkey Sanctuary, Nr Sidmouth, 01395 578222; Manor Mill (NT), 01297 680333/680481; Pecorama Model Railway and Gardens, Beer, 01297 21542; Seaton Tramway, 01297 20375

Possible birds include: Blackbird, buzzard, carrion crow, chiffchaff, cormorant, fulmar, goldfinch, green woodpecker, gulls of various hue, house martin, house sparrow, jackdaw, kestrel, linnet, magpie, peregrine falcon, raven, robin, shag, swallow, woodpigeon, wren, yellowhammer

Authors' tip: Allow time to explore Branscombe with its pretty gardens and chocolate box cottages. It is one of the longest villages in the country

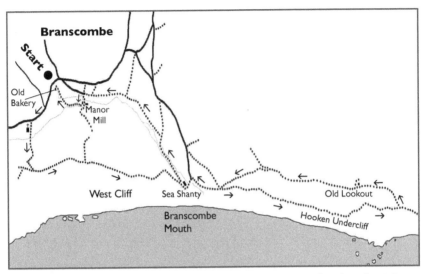

From the car park turn right along the lane, passing the thatched forge on your right and tea gardens on your left. Follow the lane uphill to the church where a footpath sign directs you through the gates and into the churchyard. Follow the tarmac path round the church and as you reach the building you will see a trodden path leading left off the church path, away from the church and between the graves and yew trees. Follow this for less than 100m to a stile which leads out of the churchyard.

About 30m from the stile cross the footbridge and follow the path uphill through the field, heading towards the tree-line with the field boundary on your right. At the trees you will find another stile leading into the woods. Cross this and ascend the steps beyond as they wind up through the trees to another stile. Beyond this turn left, still going slightly uphill under the trees. There is a fence to your left.

You ascend to reach a broad crossing path, the coast path. Go left along it – although you can't see it yet the sea is to your right. You reach a wooden kissing gate and a sign stating that you are now entering the National Trust land of West Cliff. Continue ahead, ignoring the stile to your left after the kissing gate. In about 150m the path emerges from trees. Continue in the same direction across the top of the field with lovely views down to your left across the valley and village. The path re-enters trees and you pass through another kissing gate, still on the coast path.

When you reach a right fork keep ahead unless you wish to go right to the viewpoint – but if you do be cautious as it is a precipitous drop. The coast path starts to descend and in another 50m ignore the left turn and keep ahead. You soon emerge from the trees and have your first massive view across Branscombe Mouth. Keep descending with the path, which becomes wooden-edged steps making the descent slightly easier.

The steps drop to a crossing path, turn right and immediately left to another kissing gate – you are basically heading in the same direction all the way through this section. Beyond the kissing gate walk down the field in a straight line, the sea still to your right, towards a substantial house below you. At the bottom of the field you reach a gateway on the right into the next field. Go through here and head diagonally left down the field, towards the sea and the buildings of the Sea Shanty – your first opportunity to pause for refreshment.

From the Sea Shanty cross the footbridge over the river, or wade through the ford as the mood takes you, and then pass through a kissing gate on the right with a fingerpost directing you towards Beer, two miles away.

Walking the coast path towards the Hooken Undercliff from Branscombe Mouth

The Sea Shanty

View over Branscombe

(Don't get excited, Beer is the name of the village.) The area through which you are walking is East Cliff. Follow the path towards Beer, heading up to a gate above you, the sea is still to your right. The path climbs to meet a concrete track leading you into the beautifully-located and sensitively laid-out Sea Shanty Caravan Park. Enter this and walk ahead on the main track through the site until, just over 100m from the entrance, you find a narrow footpath going right – this is the coast path towards Beer that will now take you through the remarkable habitat of the Hooken Undercliff. You will have occasional glimpses of the sea to your right but glance up to the left from time to time, to the magnificent cliffs towering above you – all part of the Jurassic Coast and the haunt of the peregrine falcon.

The undulating path through the Undercliff continues for almost a mile and towards its end glance back at the cliffs under which you've walked for a good view of an elevated cave with its petrified guardian. The path starts to ascend and becomes stepped. The steps gradually leading you left up the cliff – don't go right as that leads to a sudden drop. Follow the steps and path uphill, until you eventually emerge from the Undercliff area at a kissing gate and a three-way fingerpost.

Beer is to the right and there is a separate walk in the book for that area. Our way goes left after the kissing gate, back across the top of the Hooken Cliffs towards Branscombe Mouth. This is a lovely stretch of walking, high above the sea. Go through another gate and beyond this you pass an old lookout with an adjacent cottage. Here you will see a bridleway heading inland but you keep ahead on the path with the sea to your left. (The public path to Branscombe Mouth from this lookout is actually about 30m further over beside the right hand fence, but walkers mostly keep straight ahead, hugging the line of the cliff – but not too literally.)

Beyond the old lookout, at the end of the field, pass through two gates in quick succession to re-enter the National Trust land of East Cliff. Follow the clear path beyond and within 150m you will see a wooden post showing that a bridleway diverges to the right, but the footpath you need is straight on, dropping down into the valley with the Sea Shanty below you and the village of Branscombe inland behind it.

You reach a fingerpost with diminutive fingers sporting the coast path acorn sign. From here head down the steps to a stile, knees firmly in gear, and keep descending to cross the concrete track to the caravan park, retracing your steps to the Sea Shanty. From this point walk round the back of the building and turn right, looking for the sign that points you to Branscombe Village, 0.6 mile away. This is where you are heading.

This is an attractive, well-surfaced path which takes you over a footbridge, continuing towards Branscombe Village, as shown on the four-way post just after the bridge. About 700m from the footbridge you reach some barns where the path emerges near another four-way fingerpost. Here go left shown as 'public footpath link to coast path'. Within 50m you reach the National Trust's Manor Mill. Here, walk between the buildings and go through the second small gate on the right, adjacent to the buildings. This is now all National Trust land.

Walk through the field with the stream to your left, passing through a double gate over a footbridge. At the end of the next small field pass through another gate and cross another bridge. This well-trodden path leads you through a series of small fields and across rivulets until you find yourself walking through a tranquil orchard to arrive at the lovely Old Bakery Tea Rooms and Gardens, again all owned by the National Trust. This is an excellent spot to refresh after your walk and is just across the lane from the Village Hall Car Park from whence you started.

The Hooken Undercliff

This remarkable area was formed when about 10 acres of the cliff slumped towards the sea one night in 1790. The land dropped over 200 feet (60m) resulting in the prominent chalk pinnacles and tangled remains of what had been clifftop fields and hedges. The seaward pressure of the slip caused a reef to rise just  off the coast and it was said that lobster pots, placed in the water the previous day, could be seen raised up out of the water along this reef. During the 19thC the area was used to cultivate potatoes.

Walk 2
Beer
Distance: 1¾ miles / 2.9km

This is a very short walk on good paths with lovely views. It explores a section of the Jurassic Coast (see feature on Otterton walk), the very pretty village of Beer and the environs of the village that visitors might otherwise miss. It is also an opportunity to call into Seaton if you wish to extend the walk. Be prepared for some uphill bits!

Map: OS Explorer 116, Lyme Regis & Bridport

Start point: Cliff Top Car Park, Beer. Post code: EX12 3AQ. Grid Ref: SY228888

Directions to start: Beer is reached on the B3174, signed off the A3052 east of Sidmouth

Parking: Cliff Top Car Park. Post code: EX12 3AQ

Public Transport: Bus operators that pass through Beer are: First in Dorset & South Somerset and Axe Valley Mini-Travel. Timetables available online at www.travelinesw.com. Nearest railway stations are Axminster (6.8 miles) and Honiton (7.9 miles)

Distance: 1¾ miles

Refreshments: Anchor Inn, Beer, 01297 20386; Cliffside Cabin, Seaton Hole, Seaton (no tel). There are numerous other places to eat in both Beer and Seaton. Chapple's, Ducky's and Kenno's Beach cafés, are all well-situated on Beer Beach, but bear in mind that they are seasonal

Toilets: Above the beach in Beer and near Cliffside Cabin in Seaton

Nearby places to stay: Bay View Guest House, Beer: 01297 20489; Colebrooke House, Beer, 01297 20308

Nearby places of interest: Beer Quarry Caves, 01297 680282; Branscombe Forge (NT), 01297 680333/680481; The Donkey Sanctuary, Nr Sidmouth, 01395 578222; Lyme Bay Winery, 01297 551355; Pecorama Model Railway and Gardens, 01297 21542; Seaton Tramway, 01297 20375

Possible birds include: Buzzard, collared dove, grey wagtail, gulls of various hue, magpie, pheasant, pied wagtail, raven, woodpigeon, wren

Authors' tip: We cannot recommend highly enough the hire of stripy deckchairs on Beer Beach, conveniently in front of all the beach cafés. It's a wonderful way to unwind and feels very 'English' – but leave the knotted hankies behind

---

First of all enjoy the view from this elevated car park – you can see across to Seaton in the bay, beyond which the coastline stretches to Dorset. On

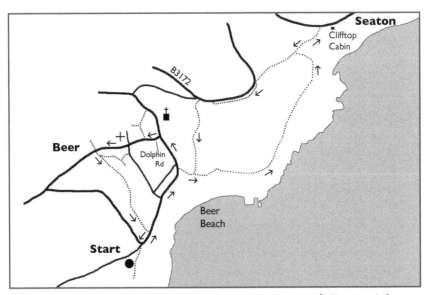

a clear day the Isle of Portland is visible. Walk downhill out of the car park to join the lane going down into Beer. This takes you past a descending terrace of very attractive cottages before bringing you to the road outside the Anchor Inn. Sea Hill, leading to the beach, goes down to the right, but the walk goes straight across to a two-way fingerpost and follows the direction towards Seaton. Within a few metres you pass public toilets on the left and beyond here go up steps to a three-way fingerpost. Keep on along the coast path towards Seaton. The sea is to your right and the path climbs up through the trees. Where there are steps look out for the decorative stones in the risers and pause occasionally to admire the views – there are benches!

Follow this path for 700m until it emerges onto a narrow tarmac lane. Here you have options. If you wish to explore Seaton and partake at the Clifftop Cabin, 100m away, go right, but then come back to this point afterwards. The walk goes left, uphill along the narrow lane. As you reach the main road turn left and immediately right along the permissive bridleway to Beer, the hedge is to your right (hiding the road) with a field and sea views to your left. The bridleway emerges onto the road. Turn left, watching out for traffic, and in 50m you find a public footpath leading left, signposted for Jubilee Gardens. Take this, avoiding walking

Attractive cottages descending into Beer

Beer Beach

into anyone's private garden, and keep ahead for about 60m at which point you will see a yellow-arrowed path descending to the right, go down here. The path becomes stepped and leads you back into the village. At the bottom of the steps walk towards the Anchor Inn then turn right to walk along the main village street – a delightful area with its fast-flowing leat, flower-fringed in summer, and some very attractive buildings.

Turn left beside the Dolphin Hotel – this road appears to be called both Dolphin Road and Clapps Lane according to the road sign. It's actually the former and it runs into the latter. Keep straight ahead as the road goes uphill and becomes Clapps Lane. The road passes a chapel and its surrounding graveyard on the right, designated as a 'living churchyard and wildlife sanctuary'. Just beyond the end of the churchyard turn left off Clapps Lane (there is a footpath sign attached to the wall rather than on a fingerpost) passing houses called Higher Meadow and Lane Head and walking uphill. Keep ahead as the path narrows, but just before you enter the narrow bit enjoy the view left across the roofscape of Beer towards the parish church. The narrow, fenced path goes between gardens and views along the coast open up. The path emerges at a road, turn right and within 100m you are back at the car park from which you set off.

Beer Stone
Beer is famous for its beautiful creamy-grey stone which was quarried in this area from Roman times. A soft stone, which hardens when exposed to the air after quarrying, it has been used extensively in the region's buildings including Exeter Cathedral where the screen of the West Front is comprised of Beer stone. It also appears further afield – in over 20 British cathedrals, the Tower of London and Windsor Castle to name just some buildings where it has been used. The Beer Quarry caves are the oldest continuously worked industrial site in the country and are a monument to the quarrying techniques of successive ages, the architectural style of different periods being reflected in the way the caves were constructed during the mining of that time. They are a Site of Special Scientific Interest (SSSI). The caves have also served as a place for cultivating mushrooms.

Walk 3
Blackborough
Distance: 3½ miles / 5.6km

This walk on the edge of the Blackdowns offers great variety – glorious views, lovely field paths, woodland tracks and some rather curious history. Be prepared for several ascents and muddy areas after wet weather but don't be put off – it's one of our favourite walks and is good for summer butterflies such as speckled woods.

Map: OS Explorer 128, Taunton & the Blackdown Hills

Start point: North end of the village near the site of the former church. Post code: EX15 2HJ. Grid ref: ST094092

Directions to start: Blackborough is a hamlet lying 6 miles NE of Cullompton. It is situated north of the A373 Cullompton to Honiton road and can be accessed via country lanes

Parking: There are usually spaces by the site of the former church. Post code: EX15 2HJ

Public Transport: Although no buses pass through Blackborough the following operators run services that stop at nearby villages: Dartline Coaches, Redwoods Travel, Stagecoach South West. Timetables available online at www.travelinesw.com. Nearest railway stations are Tiverton Parkway (4.3 miles) and Feniton (5.9 miles)

Distance: 3½ miles

Refreshments: Ashill Inn, Ashill, 01884 840506; Keepers Cottage, Nr Kentisbeare, 01884 266247; Wyndham Arms, High St, Kentisbeare, 01884 266327

Toilets: None en route

Nearby places to stay: Forest Glade Holiday Park, Nr Blackborough, 01404 841381; The Old Vicarage B&B, Broadhembury, 01404 841648; Orway Crescent Farm B&B, Orway, Kentisbeare, 01884 266876

Nearby places of interest: Coldharbour Mill, Uffculme, 01884 840960; Escot Park, Ottery St. Mary, 01404 822188

Possible birds include: Blackbird, blue tit, buzzard, carrion crow, chaffinch, chiffchaff, collared dove, goldfinch, great tit, house martin, jackdaw, magpie, mallard, mistle thrush, pheasant, raven, rook, swallow, willow warbler, woodpigeon, wren

Authors' tip: If you'd like one more fabulous view before going home turn right (at ** in the text below) to follow an ancient, mossy beech boundary on the left. You're climbing here but beyond the boundary the path soon flattens out before bearing right to wind amongst the trees to a forestry gate. Go right at the gate to reach a tree-enclosed trig point and continue beyond it to emerge from the trees into a viewpoint with a well-located bench on the left. Sit down

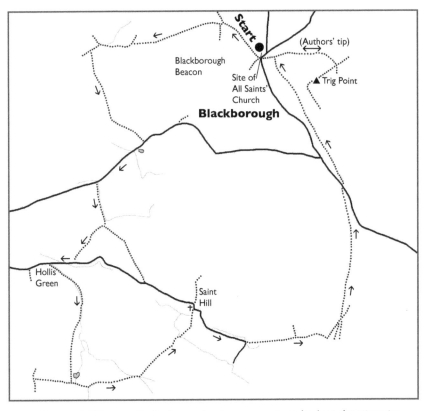

and savour it. When you've had enough retrace your steps back to the trig point and the forestry gate. From here go left on the path to then descend beside the beech boundary all the way back to your start point

Visit the churchyard then exit the gate and turn sharp right to follow the marked footpath along the track beside the churchyard. The hill to your left is Blackborough Beacon, once forming part of the communication system that warned of the approach of the Spanish Armada (see feature on East Budleigh Common walk). There are distant views to your right here towards Culmstock Beacon and on a clear day you can make out the hut at the summit – imagine the chain of beacon fires that would once have lit the night sky.

The track you are following leads to Blackborough House but before you get there, about 200m from the start, you find a footpath going left. Take

Descending from Blackborough

this, entering a field from where there is a rather arresting view towards the chimneys of Blackborough House. Walk through the field in the direction of the footpath arrow, passing, just as you enter the field, two gates and another footpath on the left that you don't want. The footpath you need goes straight down the field – the left hand boundary wanders away from you and as you progress there is a lovely woodland to your right. You are walking into a magnificent view.

This line crosses through an old boundary of trees – a post with a yellow arrow reassures you that you're on the right path. Continue beyond this down to the bottom of the field where you will find a gate with two yellow arrows and a small bridge crossing a stream. After the bridge your way lies to the left – a path rich with wild garlic in spring. Continue beneath the trees, looking out for a footpath sign about 150m from the bridge that directs you left at a fork in the path. Go left here and within 50m look out for a stile on the left leading up from the path and into a field.

Walk across the field, the boundary is to your right, and you reach a gate with a small footbridge followed by another gate. From here go up into the field as the arrow directs and head straight across to another boundary with a field gate. Go through the gate and turn left (the footpath arrow here is slightly misleading) to follow the hedge on your left towards a farm. At the end of the field emerge through a gate onto a track, passing barns on the left and keeping straight ahead to the lane.

Turn right along the lane for about 250m after which you find a stile on the left. Cross this and walk through the field with the hedge to your left. At the end you find another stile on the left. Cross it and go immediately right through a gate then immediately right again to follow the field boundary on your right. (In effect this series of turns means you are walking at roughly 90° to your direction through the previous field.) Leave the field over a stile onto the lane and turn right.

About 100m along the lane, by a house called Hollis Green, a footpath goes left into a field. Take this and follow the direction of the sign along the right hand boundary of the field with lovely views to the left. Keep your eyes open for a stile on the right after about 250m that leads to a footbridge over the stream. Cross this and then another stile, then walk through the next field – a yellow arrow directs you to go diagonally left but if there are crops you will need to walk round the left hand boundary until you reach a kissing gate. Go through the gate and walk straight ahead through the next small field with a boundary ditch and a few coppiced trees on your left.

A gate at the end leads out to a track with a three-way fingerpost. Go left here, passing the buildings of Lower Henland Farm. About 200m beyond

One of many sweeping views on this walk

All Saints Church

All Saints Church was built in 1838, in the Early English style, by the 4th (and final) Earl of Egremont. It had an octagonal spire and was a distinctive landmark. Although in use until the late 20thC its exposed position rendered it structurally unsafe and it was demolished in the 1990s. The churchyard is still well-maintained and can be beautiful with wild flowers in spring. Blackborough House was also built in 1838 by the earl, half the building being the home of the then rector of All Saints, the earl's cousin. A footpath passes through the environs of this remarkable house but at the time of writing the premises were in use as scrapyards. The route we have chosen avoids the rather eerie bits and just provides a striking view of very impressive chimneys – what's below them is left to your imagination. The house is privately owned and lived in.

the house and barns the track leads you to a fingerpost directing you left over a small bridge with a gate beyond. After this the footpath goes diagonally right across the field to the far corner but at the time of writing there were crops planted and provision had been made to walk round two sides of the field, following the right hand boundary. This is a more polite thing to do in the circumstances. There are lovely views to the left from here.

In the corner a stile leads onto a path which crosses a plank bridge and passes cottages to emerge at a lane between Saint Hill Baptist Church and the church hall. Turn right along the lane. This is uphill! Keep going, and the lane becomes a track. After 500m you pass a footpath on the left. This path is not for you – but there is a very acceptable bench beside it inviting you to 'rest awhile'. Long may it remain there. Keep going up until you reach the well-named Prospect House on the right. Beyond it the way enters woods. Turn left on the public bridleway under the trees. In about 50m the path forks. Take the right hand option and go uphill for less than 100m to a three-way fingerpost beyond which you can see another fingerpost about 20m away. Go left at the first post and keep ahead on this broad, level woodland track. (Don't be tempted to veer off to the right on a different, uphill bridleway that is indicated from the further fingerpost. If you're out of breath you're on the wrong path.) Your way lies along a lovely, fairly flat, stony track. The woodland rises steeply to your right and beyond the trees to your left you can, if the leaves aren't too dense, just about discern open fields as the land drops away.

Follow this track for 250m until you reach a lane. Cross over and take the public footpath opposite which climbs through the trees before levelling out to wend its elevated way above the lane which is down to your left. This is a delightful path, keep along it enjoying some lovely trees. The path enters amongst, then soon emerges from, conifers. Keep going and you start to descend bearing slightly left. (If you notice the indistinct right fork don't take it.)

You drop to another three-way fingerpost and those who wish to follow the authors' tip (**) should now refer to that in the intro information to this walk. Those who wish to return straight to their car go left at the fingerpost and you soon find yourself back at the churchyard.

Which way?

Walk 4
Gittisham
Distance: 2.6 miles / 4.2km

A short, easy walk from one of the most attractive villages in East Devon, with just one noticeably uphill section. Following field footpaths and shady woodland lanes this is a little gem if you only want a brief excursion. The lanes are quiet so traffic is unlikely to pose a problem.

Map: OS Explorer 115, Exmouth & Sidmouth 1:25 000

Start point: The village green by the church. Post code: EX14 3AJ. Grid ref: SY133984

Directions to start: The village of Gittisham lies 2½ miles to the south west of Honiton and can be reached from the A375 along a country lane

Parking: On road parking in the centre of the village

Public Transport: Bus operators that pass through Gittisham are: Stagecoach Devon and Dartline Coaches. Timetables available online at www.travelinesw.com. Nearest railway station is Honiton (2.2 miles)

Distance: 2.6 miles

Refreshments: Hare and Hounds, Putts Corner, Sidbury, 01404 41760, Toast, 155 High St, Honiton, 01404 598067

Toilets: None en route

Nearby places to stay: Splatthayes B&B, Buckerell, 01404 850464

Nearby places of interest: Allhallows Museum of Lace and Local Antiquities, High St, Honiton, 01404 44966; Escot Park, Ottery St. Mary, 01404 822188

Possible birds include: Blackbird, blue tit, buzzard, carrion crow, chaffinch, chiffchaff, collared dove, goldfinch, great tit, house martin, house sparrow, jackdaw, pheasant, pied wagtail, willow warbler, swallow, woodpigeon

Authors' tip: Allow time to admire the photogenic village of Gittisham with its clusters of picture-perfect thatched cottages. And, if you're feeling flush, perhaps treat yourselves to a meal at Combe House

---

From the village green outside the church you will see the stone School House with an adjacent public footpath. Take this, passing houses on the left, beyond which the path narrows. A kissing gate leads into a field. Follow the boundary on your right and within 200m you will find a gate leading to a footbridge on the right. Cross the bridge, noting the yellow arrow on it and follow the line indicated diagonally across the field beyond. This line leads to a farm gate with a kissing gate beside it that

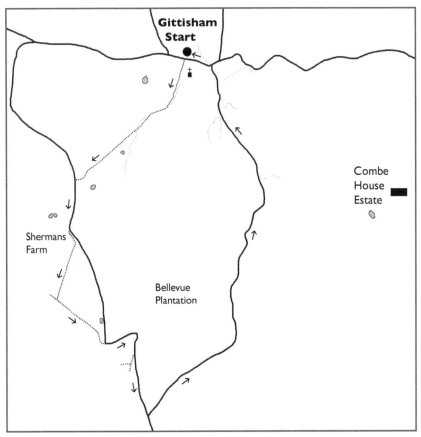

has an arrow (make sure you get the right gate!). Pass through and turn right to follow the boundary on your right all the way to the corner of the field where you emerge onto a lane.

Turn left along the lane for 200m until you reach Shermans Farm. Here, within the entrance to the farm on the right, you will see a footpath fingerpost directing you past some barns. Follow this line keeping the barns to your right and at their end you will find a stile with a yellow arrow. Cross here and go diagonally right across the field towards a thatched farmhouse in the distance, passing between two prominent trees. There are expansive views to your right here and up to your left is the wooded ridge of Bellevue Plantation through which the walk passes later. This line reaches a metal gate, go left beyond it on the bridleway,

Majestic trees

ascending towards the woods. Once you reach the trees pause to look behind you at the thirst-quenching view, then go left with the track to enter amongst the trees. A few more metres brings you to the lane.

Turn right along the lane which immediately swings left, going uphill for 150m. It then bends right and starts to level off – and the tough bit is now over. Keep along the lane and as it begins to gently drop after about 350m you will find a left turning, still in the woodland. Go left here along this lovely sylvan lane, noticing the ancient, tree-topped boundary that flanks the road. Look up occasionally, there are some majestic trees around here which are beautiful in sunlight and are part of the estate surrounding Combe House. As the lane drops and leaves the woodland, before entering the

Combe House & Gittisham

The history of the village and the manor of Combe have been intertwined since around the 12thC when the whole estate was owned by the De Lumine family. Over successive centuries the estate passed between various owners, either by inheritance or purchase. From the 17thC it was under the ownership  of the Putt family and it was Tom Putt who planted Bellevue Plantation, during the middle of the 18thC. Through marriage, the Marker family took ownership in the mid 19thC and still own the property today, although part of the village has now been sold away from the estate. Combe House was hard to maintain as a family home and from the 1960s was leased out, and is now managed as a splendid country house hotel and restaurant.

village, you have a rather splendid view across the parkland towards this stately pile.

Keep following the lane past Catshayes Farm on the right. You eventually cross the stream and then follow this on your left to arrive back in the village centre and your start point.

Gittisham

Walk 5
Tipton St. John & Venn Ottery
Distance: 4¾ miles / 7.6km

This is a really good walk of lovely contrasts: tranquil river valleys, ancient green lanes, historic churches and fabulous views. The bird life is good so it may be an idea to take binoculars with you. The terrain is quite easy with just a couple of brief uphill stretches. It can be muddy after wet weather but it never went over our boots! Part of the walk follows the Coleridge link footpath, a route linking Tipton St. John with Ottery St. Mary and Harpford, Samuel Taylor Coleridge having been born in Ottery.

Map: OS Explorer 115, Exmouth & Sidmouth 1:25 000

Start point: Centre of Tipton St. John. Post code: EX10 0AA. Grid ref: SY091197

Directions to start: Tipton St. John is south of Ottery St. Mary off the A30

Parking: On road in the village – please be considerate towards residents

Public Transport: Bus operators that pass through Tipton St. John & Venn Ottery are: Stagecoach Devon and Dartline Coaches. Timetables available online at www.travelinesw.com. Nearest railway station is Honiton (2.2 miles)

Distance: 4¾ miles

Refreshments: Golden Lion, Tipton St. John, 01404 812881 (see tip below)

Toilets: None en route

Nearby places to stay: Higher Coombe Farm, Tipton St. John, 01404 813385; Lancercombe Farm, Tipton St. John, 01404 81286

Nearby places of interest: Escot Park, Ottery St. Mary, 01404 822188

Possible birds include: Blackbird, carrion crow, cormorant, gulls of various hue, hobby, house martin, little grebe, pheasant, jay, sand martin, swallow, woodpigeon, wren

Authors' tip: If you are planning to visit the Golden Lion please bear in mind that they don't like muddy boots! Have something to change into or make sure there are no holes in your socks

Walk along the lane passing the Golden Lion on your right and within 100m you will find a footpath signed on the left, take this, a narrow path which brings you to a stile. Cross this and continue – it can be muddy along here! Cross a second stile and keep going, the narrow path opens up into a field. Walk straight ahead on the well-trodden path, as directed by a yellow arrow on a post. To your left as you enter the field you will see the arches of an old railway bridge over the River Otter, the railway

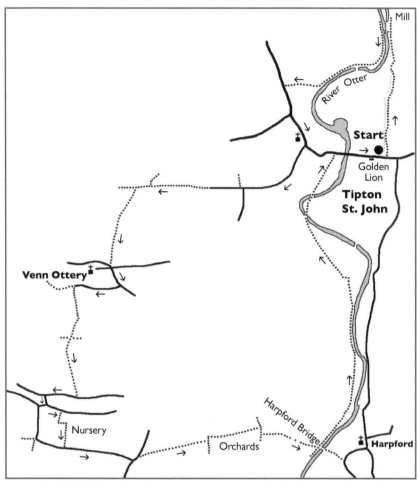

closed in 1967. The river is some way to your left although from time to time you will have a small stream immediately on your left. At the end of the field pass through a metal gate and keep going in the same direction, passing through occasional gates, until the path leads you to the buildings of an old mill, just over 600m from the village. The mill buildings were in the process of being renovated when we were there.

Near the mill you find a footbridge spanning the river, cross here and as you come down off the bridge go fully left again, so that the river is still to your left. Within 30m pass through the remains of an old field boundary, after which cross the field towards the end of the old railway bridge ahead. At the bridge walk straight past it to cross the line of the old railway and continue in the same direction, the river to your left. You are heading towards houses on the outskirts of Tipton St. John.

Follow the river to reach a gate out of the field – another potentially muddy area. Beyond this bear right to walk under the trees on a clear path. This leads you to the lane into the village. Turn left along it and ignore the first right turn, Metcombe Vale, keeping ahead on the road which passes the elevated church of St. John the Evangelist. This is worth a visit for its lovely windows and attractive reredos screen. Return to the road through the gate at the lower, far end of the churchyard and turn immediately right on the lane for Venn Ottery and Newton Poppleford.

This quiet lane bends right and climbs for a short way. Follow it past the village sign for Venn Ottery (from 'Fenotri', meaning marshy place by the River Otter) and as the lane bends sharp left keep ahead on a drive that says 'unsuitable for motors', ignoring the bridleway to the right. The drive leads past houses and then becomes a track, climbing gently. After

River Otter

St. John the Evangelist

400m ignore another bridleway on the right and take the left turn about 60m further along. You're quite high now so can enjoy good views from gateways. The track descends, ignore a right hand track and keep straight on. Walking this in late summer the ground was littered with unripe hazelnuts, which suggests good dormouse territory, although not surprisingly we didn't see any.

The track brings you to Venn Ottery, keep straight ahead along the lane opposite the path you emerged from, passing Barton Mews on the right. (If you wish to visit the tiny church of St. Gregory with its 12thC tower go down Barton Mews to reach it.) Just over 100m along the lane you find a right turn signed as 'unmetalled', although it is tarmac at this point. Take this, passing a few houses, and keep ahead for just over 200m until you reach an isolated house on the left. Turn left here, a weathered sign (it was weathered when we were there) tells you that this is Wayside.

Beyond the house the path climbs between hedges, again it can be muddy. Keep on this path, ignoring any side turnings for almost 600m until you reach the lane opposite a house called Harleyford. Turn right along the lane and in 150m go left by some thatched cottages then left again in another 40m. Notice the lovely rounded pebbles in the wall here, which came from the East Devon Pebblebeds.

Within 100m you find a footpath over a stile on the right. Take this and walk ahead with the boundary to your right. Within 50m you see a yellow-arrowed post, turn left here and in about 30m the path goes sharp right again. You are walking through an orderly nursery. You soon reach another arrowed post, the arrow pointing obliquely left although the well-trodden path goes straight ahead. Follow the path and in less than 100m you reach a stile onto the lane. Turn left, this is the East Devon Way.

Follow the lane – at the right time of year you will see some pretty cottage gardens along here. You reach a T-junction with the entrance to the nursery on your left. Go left along the lane for 15m then turn right through a gate with a footpath sign and a nice, pink East Devon Way arrow pointing you on your way. Walk ahead as it directs between hedges and as the field opens up bear right to follow its right hand boundary uphill. Enjoy the views to your left as you climb.

You reach a stile, keep straight ahead beyond it as the arrow shows, following the line of tall trees with orchards on either side – this bit of the walk is a real treat! You reach a footpath T-junction with a view ahead towards Harpford. Go left for 30m then turn right down steps – this is still the East Devon Way. Follow the path gently downhill to a kissing

East Devon Pebblebeds

In this area one frequently finds attractive, rounded stones on the ground or used in building. These come from the East Devon 'pebblebeds' which consist of ancient layers of even older pebbles, lying below heathland formed during the Triassic era (250–200 million years ago). Then the climate and lie of the land were very different, Britain still being physically connected to mainland Europe. The pebbles were formed in a desert region with a mighty river flowing through it that carried the stones along, tumbling them into their rounded shape. Fossils in some of the pebbles show that they came from northern France. The pebbles are also known as 'popples' from which Newton Poppleford derives its name.

gate. Descend the steps beyond here (use the hand rail!) and at the bottom of the steps go right, walking through trees. Don't trip over the roots.

You soon reach more steps, after them go left to cross a footbridge and emerge into a field. Bear slightly right across the field, towards the right of Harpford church tower and to where another footbridge leads out of the field. It was across this stretch that we watched a hobby chasing house martins. Cross the footbridge and follow the short path to another kissing gate – here you are once more crossing the old railway line. After the kissing gate go left through the field with the fence to your left.

At the end of the field you reach Harpford Bridge. If you wish to visit the village cross the river, but otherwise go left, with the River Otter on your right. You reach a kissing gate, pass through into the next huge field. Follow the well-trodden path, the field boundary, with the river beyond, to your right. Occasionally the river meanders off but keep going through the field on the path until you reach the road. Cross over, looking out for traffic and turn right along the pavement. The road crosses the river and leads you back into the centre of the village from which you started, passing the Golden Jubilee Clock on the way – a decorative finish.

Descending through orchards on the East Devon Way

Walk 6
Budleigh Salterton
Distance: 2¼ miles / 3.6km

This is a lovely, easy walk across varied terrain with superb views and is good for butterflies in summer. It's a must if you want to stretch your legs and don't have much spare time. There is one very brief ascent along the coast path.

Map: OS Explorer 115, Exmouth & Sidmouth 1:25 000	
Start point: Links Road, Budleigh Salterton. Post code: EX9 6DF. Grid ref: SY053819	
Directions to start: Budleigh Salterton is a small town which lies equidistant between Exmouth and Sidmouth on the south coast. It can be accessed from the A3052 via the B3178 at Newton Poppleford	
Parking: On Links Road – this is a wide, residential road but please park courteously and don't block anyone's drive	
Public Transport: Bus operators that pass through Budleigh Salterton are: Stagecoach Devon and Axe Valley Mini-Travel. Timetables available online at www.travelinesw.com. Nearest railway station is Exmouth (4.1 miles)	
Distance: 2¼ miles	
Refreshments: The Feathers Hotel, 35, High St, Budleigh Salterton, 01395 442042; Oak Barn Coffee Shop, Oak Barn Furnishings, Knowle Hill, Budleigh Salterton, 01395 446484	
Toilets: None en route	
Nearby places to stay: Lavender House, 9 Moorlands Rd, Budleigh Salterton, 01395 446195; Pebbles B&B, 16 Fore St, Budleigh Salterton, 01395 442417; Stoneborough House B&B, 21a East Budleigh Rd, Budleigh Salterton, 01395 445923	
Nearby places of interest: A la Ronde (NT), Summer Lane, Exmouth, 01395 265514; Fairlynch Museum, 27 Fore St, Budleigh Salterton, 01395 442666	
Possible birds include: Blackbird, blue tit, buzzard, carrion crow, chaffinch, chiffchaff, collared dove, goldfinch, great tit, house martin, house sparrow, jackdaw, pheasant, pied wagtail, willow warbler, swallow, woodpigeon	
Authors' tip: One of the authors is a keen golfer and advises that courtesy should be exercised around the golf course. If someone is about to take a shot stand still until they have done so and don't let your dog pinch the golf balls – the owners can get touchy	

Walk down Links Road towards the main road and turn left along it for a mere 10m to where you will find a footpath going left. This is signed as Littleham Church Path. Take this and beyond the houses it becomes a

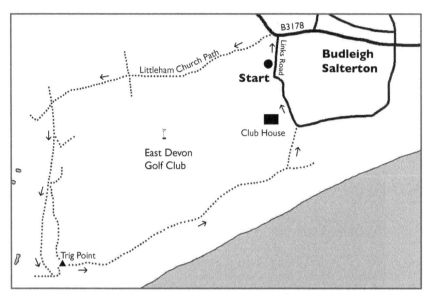

pleasant, narrow path under trees. At a crosspaths keep ahead as shown by the yellow arrow and follow the path along the periphery of the golf course to reach a gate. Beyond the gate walk ahead through the field with the boundary to your right and beautiful views beyond it.

After almost 250m you reach a four-way fingerpost. Keep ahead on the Littleham Church Path, you will soon find yourself walking across the middle of the field, although there once was a hedge along this stretch. At the far side you rise to meet a kissing gate. A yellow arrow here directs you beyond the gate across the golf course, heading for a black and white post within 100m at the edge of the trees – you're crossing the fairway here so watch out for missiles. Under the trees you meet a footpath going left and right. Turn left and within about 30m Littleham Church Path goes right but you now keep ahead towards West Down Beacon.

The path emerges from the trees onto the golf course once more. Keep straight ahead in the same direction, ignoring the almost immediate left fork and within about 100m you will find a three-way fingerpost. Keep straight on as directed for West Down Beacon, passing a bunker to your right and reaching a yellow-arrowed post by the 9th tee – this is within approximately 200m of emerging from the trees. Here bear right in the direction of the arrow and in about 50m you reach another three-way fingerpost. Here take the option for Exmouth leaving, for the moment, the path to West Down Beacon.

This narrow path brings you to a kissing gate leading into a field, through which you follow the left hand boundary towards the sea with gorgeous views to the right across Exmouth – if the light is good look out for the church tower, poking up like Batman from amongst the houses. Rather closer to hand you can see the church at Littleham. A holiday park comes into view above Straight Point and soon you reach the coast path along the clifftop. Turn left, pass through a kissing gate, enjoy the views and then climb up past a bench to reach a three-way fingerpost. This is West Down and up to the left you will see the trig point of West Down Beacon. It's worth climbing up to this to enjoy the vast panorama along the Jurassic Coast (see feature on Otterton walk – if you wish to explore the coast east of here you can do so on that walk).

Back at the three-way fingerpost keep on towards Budleigh Salterton, following the acorn-waymarked coast path. It starts to drop, ahead is a good view across the renowned Budleigh Salterton beach, rare for its composition of Triassic pebbles and cobbles (see feature on Tipton St. John walk). Keep on the coast path for 1km (just over ½ mile) from the trig point until you find a post with a grid ref on its badge of SY054815. From

View from West Down Beacon

here follow the yellow arrow left, away from the coast, up a few steps and along a narrow, paved path. This brings you back to the golf course with the club house over to the left. Another yellow arrow directs you straight ahead, beside the fence on the right, to meet the lane. Turn left along the lane, which is also a public footpath, and follow it until it brings you to the top of Links Road. Your car awaits.

Budleigh Salterton & Littleham Church Path

From Mediæval times Budleigh Salterton was a small fishing village called Saltre or Salterne, named for the salt pans which existed at the mouth of the River Otter to collect salt for use in preserving. Monks from Otterton Priory collected the salt which raised a high price in inland areas where it was less readily available than on the coast. Originally the village had no church of its own but was served by the church at Littleham, just over 1½ miles (2.5km) away as the crow flies. Every Sunday, whatever the weather, villagers used this path to walk to church in Littleham where, incidentally, Lady Nelson is buried. From the early 19thC Budleigh Salterton started to grow in popularity as a watering hole and the first chapel was built here in 1811. The church path remains as a lovely, historic stroll.

Looking towards Budleigh Salterton

Walk 7
East Budleigh Common
Distance: 3¼ miles / 5.2km

*This is a delightful walk on woodland tracks with sudden, surprising views –
including that of a beautiful, reflective reservoir. A lovely walk at any time of
year, we researched it for this book on a misty, autumn morning when the gorse
was festooned with dew-heavy cobwebs and 'tents' of lackey moth caterpillars.
In season, the purple heather is beautiful and as the old saying goes "when the
gorse is out of flower, kissing is out of season" and you'll get plenty of bright
yellow, coconut-fragranced blooms along the way. Also look out for damsel and
dragon flies near the damp areas. The paths can be a little muddy in places but
are easily negotiable and the ascents are gentle. Some of the paths are through
forestry plantations so you may find evidence of logging.*

Map: OS Explorer 115, Exmouth & Sidmouth 1:25 000

Start point: Car park at Grid ref: SY038843. Make sure you get the right one
– this is the most south westerly of the car parks on this lane, the one closest to
the B3179

Directions to start: From the village of East Budleigh drive west along Hayes
Lane passing Hayes Barton (Sir Walter Raleigh's birthplace) on the right. Continue
for 0.6 miles until you reach a T-junction where you turn left signed for Exmouth.
After 100m turn left and after passing a car park in 400m continue for a further
500m to reach the car park and start point on your left

Parking: Car park at Grid ref: SY038843. A little rough under-tyre. No post
code

Public Transport: Bus services that run in the East Budleigh Common area
are operated by Stagecoach Devon. Timetables available online at
www.travelinesw.com. Nearest railway station is Exmouth (4 miles)

Distance: 3¼ miles

Refreshments: Oak Barn Coffee Shop, Oak Barn Furnishings, Knowle Hill,
Budleigh Salterton, 01395 446484; Rolle Arms, East Budleigh, 01395 442012; Sir
Walter Raleigh, 22 High St, East Budleigh, 01395 442510

Toilets: None en route

Nearby places to stay: Barton House, St. John's Rd, Exmouth, 01395 276433;
Stoneborough House B&B, 21a East Budleigh Rd, Budleigh Salterton, 01395
445923

Nearby places of interest: A la Ronde (NT), Summer Lane, Exmouth, 01395
265514; World of Country Life, Sandy Bay, Westdown Lane, Littleham, Exmouth,
01395 274533

Possible birds include: Blackbird, buzzard, carrion crow, chaffinch, chiffchaff,

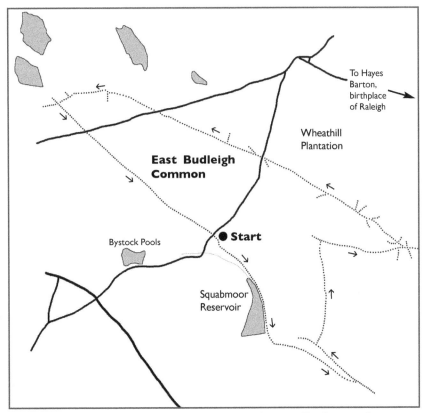

coot, goldcrest, great tit, green woodpecker, grey heron, gulls of various hue, jay, mallard, pheasant, robin, rook, stonechat, swallow, woodpigeon, wren

Authors' tip: The Devon Wildlife Trusts' Bystock Pools are situated about 500m along the lane (to the south west) from the start point, and are worth a visit for their wildlife value

The car park from which you start is situated in a woodland glade. At its entrance there is a clear two-way footpath sign. Walk away from the lane through the car park as indicated and at the far right hand end of the car park, beneath the trees, you will find the footpath. A sign telling you that you're heading for Squabmoor Reservoir plus a yellow-arrowed post 40m beyond the car park indicates that you're in the right place. Follow the narrow path as shown by the arrow, descending between gorse bushes and passing a sign stipulating that neither you nor your dogs should swim in the reservoir.

Keep on the main footpath until you reach the water's edge, 250m after leaving the car park. Continue with the reservoir, ducks and lilies over to your right, an attractive stretch of the walk. At the end of the reservoir you reach a small parking area. Cross this, ignoring the broad track that rises up to the left and looking for the yellow arrow on the post that directs you out of the car park on a path heading downhill away from the water. Initially you are walking along the left hand side of a grassy area and the path bears left about 30m from the car park to go under trees.

Keep ahead on the clear, yellow-arrowed path through the edge of light woodland, you can glimpse a field down to your right through the trees. The path emerges from the trees into an open area, keep ahead and re-enter trees on the far side. You descend to reach a stony crossing track about 600m from the end of the reservoir. Turn left along the track.

Follow this for just over 250m after which you will find a clear public footpath fingerpost on your right. Take this and follow it through a gateway within 40m, keeping ahead as directed by the yellow arrow and avoiding any temptation to veer off into fields. The track is clear with

Squabmoor Reservoir

East Budleigh Common

fields on both sides and after almost 500m it re-enters the trees and soon reaches a rather tumbledown (at the time of writing) gate and stile. Beyond here continue ahead for a few metres then turn right along a clear woodland path and follow this – there is a field beyond the trees to your right and when this field ends look out for the magnificently-rooted beech tree flanking the path.

Keep to this main path, ignoring any turns off, until it emerges at a broad crossing path on the far side of which you'll see a two-way fingerpost. Turn left along this and in just over 200m you will find a yellow-arrowed post just beyond which another oblique-crossing track is reached. Bear left along this, as directed by the arrow, climbing gently. Lovely views open up around and behind you, keep ahead ignoring any forestry tracks which lead off. About 800m from the two-way fingerpost you reach a car park with an information board about the Pebblebed Heaths (see feature on Tipton St. John walk).

Beyond the car park cross the lane and take the footpath opposite. This forks in a few metres, keep ahead, a yellow arrow directs, and a board to the right of the path denotes Clinton Devon Estates. Ignore any diverging paths and keep ahead for almost 500m from the Clinton Devon sign until you reach a crossing path, Here a narrow path goes ahead, which you don't want, and to your right is a car park area which you don't want either! Instead, go left and in about 20m turn right, along a narrow path under trees to reach the lane in about 150m.

Turn left on the lane for 20m to where it broadens out and on the right you will see a trodden path, passing through the bank boundary. (At the time of writing there was no signage.) Go through here, walking away from the lane across a small patch of ground at the far end of which a narrow path leads off. Follow this – away to the right, beyond the trees, are expansive views across quarries. Keep going on the path for about 250m. This is the East Devon Way. It passes through a footpath gate before reaching a meeting of ways with several arrows. Ignore the left hand bridleway and keep ahead on the pink-arrowed East Devon Way (which

Sir Walter Raleigh, the prominent English explorer, soldier, poet, historian, adventurer and courtier to Elizabeth I, was born in 1552 at Hayes Barton, a picturesque thatched farm (not open to the public) just to the west of East Budleigh on Hayes Lane (SY050850). Credited with introducing  potatoes and tobacco to England (although these may have been introduced earlier from the continent) he probably has quite a bit to answer for with regard to the health issues of the 21stC. Involved with the defence of Devon and Cornwall's coastline, Raleigh was instrumental in the scheme to use a chain of warning beacons when the Armada was sighted in 1588. His secret marriage in 1591 to Elizabeth Throckmorton, a lady-in-waiting to Elizabeth I, angered the jealous queen who imprisoned them both in the Tower of London. Although they were released later that year it was some time before Raleigh was back in royal favour. His eventful life ended in 1618 when he was beheaded for allegedly plotting against James I, although this was a fabrication. His embalmed head was, reputedly, presented to his wife who kept it until she died. It was later buried beside Raleigh's body in St. Margaret's Church, adjacent to Westminster Abbey.

is also a bridleway at this point). The symbol for EDW is a foxglove, which you may see carved into some of the posts. Keep ahead on the EDW for a further 270m until another meeting of ways is reached at a crosspaths, the post here has a host of arrows going in all directions. This time turn left along the blue-arrowed bridleway, leaving the EDW to continue without you.

Within 200m the bridleway brings you to a lane at another footpath gate. Cross the lane diagonally left to pick up a footpath leading downhill under trees. Follow this, keeping an eye open for yellow arrows which will direct you whenever there are options. Keep going beyond the trees, the path heading south easterly across the open common land with occasional boardwalks to help with the muddy bits and a smattering of yellow arrows to guide you. In spring, keep your eyes open for orchids. Away to your right is Squabmoor Plantation and ahead of you is the sea. After about 800m the path descends to meet the tree-line and the lane. Across this is the car park from which you started.

East Budleigh Common

Walk 8
Dalwood
Distance: 5¼ miles / 8.5km

Starting from the lovely village of Dalwood with its centuries old inn, this walk takes you on hidden ways, from the valleys of the Corry Brook and River Yarty, past romantically ruined cottages and up onto view-rich, tumbling hillsides. A must, but be prepared for some uphill stretches!

Map: OS Explorer 116, Lyme Regis & Bridport 1:25 000

Start point: Outside the lychgate of St. Peter's Church, near the war memorial. Post code: EX13 7EJ. Grid ref: ST247004

Directions to start: Dalwood is just north of the A35 Honiton to Charmouth road

Parking: On road in village – please exercise courtesy regarding people's drives

Public Transport: The 684 bus operated by Sewards Coaches serves the village (Saturdays only). Timetable available online at www.travelinesw.com. Nearest railway station is Axminster (3.2 miles)

Distance: 5¼ miles

Refreshments: Tuckers Arms, Dalwood, 01404 881342

Toilets: None en route

Nearby places to stay: Summer Lodge B&B, Dalwood, 01404 831470; Tuckers Arms, Dalwood, 01404 881342

Nearby places of interest: Burrow Farm Gardens, Dalwood, 01404 831285; Loughwood Meeting House (NT), Dalwood, 01752 346585; Lyme Bay Winery, Shute, 01297 551355; Shute Barton (NT), Shute, 01752 346585

Possible birds include: Blackbird, buzzard, carrion crow, chaffinch, chiffchaff, dipper, house martin, jackdaw, jay, pied wagtail, robin, rook, woodpigeon

Authors' tip: Do try and time your walk to take advantage of the excellent Tuckers Arms pub in the village. We did and were glad of it

---

From the church gate walk along the lane, passing the Tuckers Arms on your right and crossing the bridge over Corry Brook. Follow the lane as it bends left past the old telephone box, currently the village 'seed and plant exchange box'. Keep going on the lane, climbing out of the village for just over 500m to reach a left turn to Heathstock, which you ignore. Continue on the lane towards Axminster for another 100m to find a footpath on the left. Take this footpath, soon crossing a stile and climbing up through the field towards electricity wires.

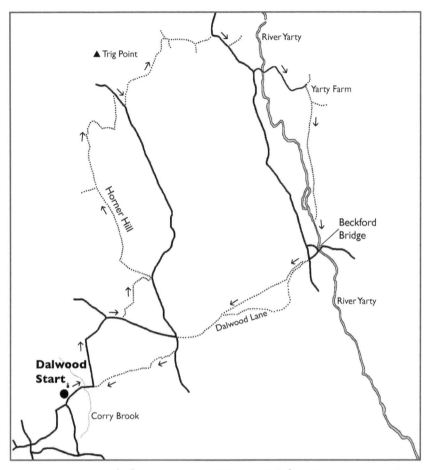

As you pass beneath the wires bear obliquely left, heading up to a yellow-arrowed post about 100m away. At this post enjoy the views behind, then follow its arrow through trees to emerge from their canopy back into the field, continuing up to a stile. Cross this and keep ahead to the left hand corner, about 50m away. Here a gate leads onto a more enclosed, sylvan path which takes you to a lane.

At the lane turn immediately left along a bridleway. Pass Hawks Hill on your left and just beyond this you find a fingerpost pointing you right, uphill on the bridleway – take this, climbing through the area of Horner Hill. This is quite a steep climb, which levels out briefly and then rises

Horner Hill

The ruined cottages you pass were inhabited until the early-mid 20thC and are now being preserved as monuments to a lifestyle long gone. A former resident, now living in a nearby village, still recalls the time when the horse-drawn baker's cart delivered bread to these cottages during the 1930s. The track you are  on, Horner Hill, was once the main lane between the villages of Stockland and Dalwood and the region around here was managed as 'turbary' – an area where peat was dug for fuel. This practice lapsed and scrub and trees took over the heathland but work is now underway to clear this and to restore the area to the rich and diverse wildlife habitat it once was. Once this is done new footpaths and information boards will be set up.

again. It levels out for a second time, enjoy this bit and keep on the main path as it forks left (the right fork can be indistinct) and starts to descend, enjoy the views through the trees.

This path drops to meet a broad crossing bridleway. Turn right here (effectively in the same direction as before) and soon you pass some ruined cottages to the right of the path. About 200m beyond here go through a broad gate and continue on the bridleway for another 200m after which bend right then left with the track, to pass through another gate. The track continues uphill under trees and goes through another gate beyond which it takes a 90° left. Keep with it. At the next gate keep ahead to meet the lane, Sandpitts is on the left. Turn right along the lane, there are great views from here, and in just over 100m you find a track signed to the left, take this and follow it for about 600m before it widens to a meeting of ways. Keep ahead here and look out for the post with two arrows that direct you to bear left downhill on a worn concrete track. The path becomes rubbly and, after about 200m, drops to meet the drive to East Horner Farm. Turn left here away from the farm entrance and keep going until you reach the lane. Turn right and follow this lane for 400m, passing Three Ashes then Cuckford Farm, before reaching a turning left signed for Yarty Farm and 'footpath to Membury'.

Take this left, crossing the River Yarty with its busy weir below the bridge. Keep going on the drive to the farm as it bends about to eventually reach the quite extensive buildings of Yarty Farm. Beyond the residential buildings on the right the lane arrives in a yard, go right on the broad track for 120m at which point the track bends left and there is a gate ahead with a yellow footpath arrow on its post. Leave the track and go through the gate to cross the field bearing slightly right as indicated. This line leads to a metal farm gate with an integral footpath gate and another arrow. Follow its direction diagonally left through the next field, heading all the way across to the furthest corner, the river hidden but down to your right as you go. In the corner you find a stile, cross and go left under the trees to a small footbridge followed by another stile. This takes you into a field, keep ahead with the river to your right and at the end of the field you reach the lane.

Turn right along the lane and bear right to cross the lovely old Beckford Bridge which dates back to the 18thC and is Grade II listed. Turn left at the end of the bridge to re-join the lane then turn right along it. You reach a T-junction with an unmetalled road opposite. Go ahead along this track,

View near Higher East Horner Farm

Beckford Bridge spans the Yarty

Dalwood Lane, and in about 30m you see a public footpath going right opposite a house. Take this footpath up the field following the left hand boundary for 310m. You are heading in the direction of a large pylon and, more importantly, a gate up ahead in the top boundary. Just prior to the woodland you reach this small gate with its footpath arrow. Don't be tempted by a larger gate prior to this. Go through the small gate and proceed for 400m in the direction of the arrow, still aiming for the pylon. At the far side of the field emerge through the arrowed gate near the pylon and rejoin the track. Enjoy the view left then turn right along the track, still going uphill. You quickly pass a pretty cottage, continue ahead away from the house along its drive until you reach the lane at Danes Hill Cross. Turn left and after 100m take the footpath right, keeping an eye open for free-range chickens.

The path leads through a gate and follows the concrete drive as it bends right. At this bend you find a footpath directed left off the drive. Take this, going downhill on a clear path which bends right to reach a stile. Cross this and go down the next field with the boundary to the right.

At the bottom pass through the gate and keep ahead beside the right hand boundary for about 30m to where you find a stile on the right. Cross this and go down the next field towards the church tower – heading for a gate at the bottom roughly below the line of the tower. This is a picturesque finish to the walk. When you reach the gate, pass through as directed by the yellow arrow and continue down keeping the hedge to the left. At the bottom leave the field via a gate on the left and turn right along the drive. This brings you to the lane by the 'phone' box. Keep ahead into the village and find your car, the Tuckers Arms and the village shop for chocolate supplies.

Heading back to Dalwood

Walk 9
Culmstock & Uffculme
Distance: 6½ miles / 10.5km

This almost entirely level walk is one of our favourites, following tranquil riverside paths and enjoying lovely views. It also has the benefit of two villages, both offering refreshment stops. The route is abundant with wildlife: as well as masses of birds it is good for butterflies (brimstone, blues, orange tip, peacock, small tortoiseshell etc.) and passes through the haunt of the elusive otter. You may see their tracks. There is some lane walking outside the villages but apart from one short stretch these are quiet backwaters with attractive houses. Some of the paths can be very muddy so wellies are advised in all but the driest of weather.

Map: OS Explorer 128, Taunton & the Blackdown Hills 1:25 000

Start point: In Culmstock by the war memorial on The Cleeve. Post code: EX15 3JH. Grid ref: ST101136

Directions to start: Culmstock is north east of Cullompton and can be accessed from the A38 via the B3391

Parking: Park in the centre of the village – there is plenty of on-road parking

Public Transport: Bus operators that pass through Culmstock are: Stagecoach South West and Redwoods Travel. Timetables available online at www.travelinesw.com. Nearest railway station is Tiverton Parkway (3.6 miles)

Distance: 6½ miles

Refreshments: Strand Stores, Culmstock, 01884 840232 (an excellent village shop and delicatessen with a wonderful café); Culm Valley Inn, Culmstock, 01884 840354; The Ostler, Commercial Rd, Uffculme, 01884 840260 – a much-loved haunt of one of the authors

Toilets: None en route

Nearby places to stay: Bowhayes Farm, Park Lane, Culmstock, 01823 680321; The Ostler Inn, Commercial Rd, Uffculme, 01884 840260; Strand Stores, The Strand, Culmstock, 01884 840232

Nearby places of interest: Coldharbour Mill, Uffculme, 01884 840960; Hemyock Castle, admin3@hemyockcastle.co.uk limited times, check before visit

Possible birds include: Blackbird, blackcap, blue tit, buzzard, carrion crow, chaffinch, chiffchaff, collared dove, dipper, dunnock, fieldfare, goldcrest, goldfinch, goosander, great spotted woodpecker, great tit, green woodpecker, greenfinch, grey wagtail, gulls of various hue, house martin, house sparrow, jackdaw, jay, kestrel, kingfisher, heron, little egret, long tailed tit, magpie, mallard, mistle thrush, nuthatch, pied wagtail, redwing, rook, sand martin, siskin, skylark, snipe, song thrush, sparrowhawk, starling, swallow, swift, treecreeper, willow warbler, woodpigeon, wren

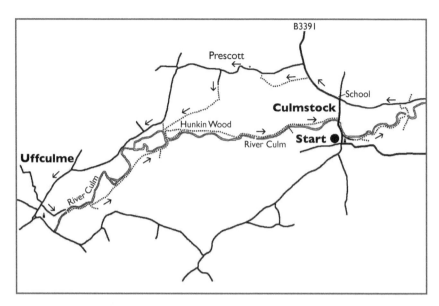

Authors' tip: If time allows consider a hike up to Culmstock Beacon on the edge of the Blackdown Hills. Situated high above the village of Culmstock at grid ref: ST I 10150, the views from here are amazing

The walk starts at the war memorial outside Strand Stores, the former post office. Walk along The Cleeve, the River Culm is to your left and beyond it there's a good view up to Culmstock Beacon on the edge of the Blackdown Hills. Pass All Saints' Church on your right and as the lane bends right keep ahead on a gravel path between pretty cottages. You reach a gate into a field. Walk through the field to the fence then turn left down the steps towards the river – don't cross the stile in the fence.

Go through the kissing gate at the bottom of the steps and turn right to walk through the field. The meandering river winds back and forth to your left through these lovely meadows, where swallow, martin and swift perform aerial acrobatics. The footpath takes a fairly direct line to a plank bridge under an oak tree. Keep going and this path will lead to another plank bridge and double gates beside an attractive 'twin' tree. From here keep ahead to the obvious footbridge.

Cross the bridge and go diagonally left through the field to the gate in the far boundary. Pass through the gate and walk diagonally left again

River Culm

up a small field to a gate leading onto a short stretch of track. This leads to a lane with the heights of Culmstock Beacon beyond. Turn left along the lane and follow it back into Culmstock, passing the converted mill with its huge wheel on the left and the village hall on the right.

You reach a junction with the school over to the right. Go straight ahead for 400m along the road to Tiverton and Wellington (Prescott Road). Watch out for traffic. This short section of the walk, from here to Oakdale Farm, doesn't last long and the route becomes appealing again beyond it. Bear with us! Pass the Culmstock village sign and keep going along the road until you find a public footpath sign pointing left into Oakdale Farm. Take this, and as the track bends left keep ahead through a gate passing barns on the left. Beyond these the track leads into an open field with a hedge to your right and lovely views around you.

At the end of the field you will find a double stile leading up through the boundary on the right. Cross here and turn left through the next field, following its left hand hedge to pass an old stone barn. Beyond this, at the end of the field, turn right, staying within the field and still keeping the hedge on your left. You quickly reach a gate onto the lane. Turn left along the lane to arrive at the hamlet of Prescott with its no-longer-used 18thC Baptist Chapel. A little further along the bendy lane passes Silverstreet Farm set back to the right. When you reach Prescott House on the right, 400m from the chapel, turn left down a 'no through road'.

This goes past the lovely Old Hall on the right, beyond it take the footpath that runs along the left side of its boundary, clearly marked with a yellow arrow. This is a delightful, narrow way that leads to a gate and a more open area. Go right in the direction of the arrow to another gate about

20m away. The tree-lined path beyond here can be deeply muddy (we did say wear wellies!!) so hang onto your sense of humour and this book and you will reach another gate into an open field. Head straight across this field as directed by the arrow. It can be marshy through here but that's as nothing compared with what you've just waded through – we were writing this during the wettest, most deeply flooded 'drought' we've ever known, hence we labour the point a bit! This marshy field can be very pretty in spring with the pink flowers of lady's smock.

You reach a gate on the far side of the field and beyond here some steps take you over a bank and through another gate. Go straight ahead after this and at the far end of the next field you find stout wooden gates. Beyond here keep going in the same direction through another field. At the end of this a small tributary of the Culm comes to meet you on the left. Near here you will find a wooden kissing gate leading into trees – pass through to enter the youthful Hunkin Wood. The water is to your left and soon the path reaches a Woodland Trust memorial bench near an information board about the woodland. This is just a taster of the area – we now leave Hunkin but you will be back later.

Culm Valley with Culmstock Beacon beyond

Looking towards Gaddon Hill from Ashley Road, Uffculme

Beyond the information board go right on the path to reach a lane, then turn left. Follow the lane past Five Fords Farm, the spire of St. Mary's Church in Uffculme comes into view ahead. You reach a T-junction. Turn left again, this is Ashley Road which takes you past houses on the outskirts of the village. Eventually you pass the primary school on your left then Clay Lane on your right. Take the next left down East Street. (Those wishing to explore the village centre should keep ahead here and rejoin us when they've finished.) Notice the huge building of the old mid 19thC brewery which is no longer in operation. Walk down East Street, continuing ahead as it runs into Kitwell Street. This bends left into Mill Street which bends right towards its end to meet the River Culm again.

Here you will find a footbridge across the river, a good point from which to see an occasional kingfisher. Cross over and turn left at the end of the bridge to walk through the field with the river on your left. At the end of the first field a kissing gate leads to a narrow path into another field. Continue through here in the same direction, the river has meandered off to your left before rejoining you further through the field. Throughout this stretch Culmstock Beacon is ahead in the distance and can look very

Hunkin Wood and Culmstock Beacon

Planted in the late 1990s as part of the Woodland Trust's Millennium Project to create community woodlands, Hunkin Wood (named after the previous landowner) contains many young alder and willow which thrive in the marshy terrain of the area. Situated on what was formerly an attractive water meadow, the planting of the woodland caused some local dissent during the early days but it is now maturing into an appealing woodland. The stone trilith faces towards Culmstock Beacon with its ancient beacon hut. The beacon formed part of an archaic communications system dating from mediæval times and was part of the chain of beacons that warned of the approach of the Spanish Armada (see also feature on East Budleigh walk).

dramatic if the light is good. At the end of the second field a double gate leads into a third field. The footpath goes straight ahead, along the line of some splendid old trees where we sometimes see a clambering treecreeper. The river ambles off again to the left and you may see walkers following its bank, but this is not the route of the public right of way.

Beyond the line of trees the river joins you again and you will find another gate at the end of the field leading into a small field. About 50m beyond here a gate brings you to a three-way fingerpost. Take the leftish option (which is in fact straight on) to cross a small footbridge. Glance right here – the development of the river meanders is very evident.

Beyond the footbridge go through another metal gate and follow the path beyond as it goes left to reach a wooden gate bringing you once more into Hunkin Wood. Another footbridge takes you over the river. This can be a lovely place of dappled light, pause awhile.

At the end of the bridge turn right to follow the path beside the river, now with the water to your right and the trees to your left. You will see an intriguing trilith to your left through the trees. Visit it, read its poem, hop through its time portal and then return to your own era and the path beside the river to continue the walk.

You emerge from the Hunkin Wood area through a wooden kissing gate. Continue in the same direction through the next three fields, the river to your right, until you reach an old, disused railway bridge spanning the river under the trees on your right. Near here a gate leads onto a clinker path – the line of the former Culm Valley Light Railway that closed to passengers in the 1960s but continued to serve the dairy in nearby Hemyock until 1975. Go through the gate and turn left away from the railway bridge. In about 50m you reach another yellow-arrowed gate into a field on the right. Enter this field and follow the footpath beside the river. Pass a footbridge without crossing and about 100m beyond bear left to join a path that is fenced from the field but still going through it. Follow this, the line of the old railway is to your left.

Beyond the next gate you have a good view of the Grade II listed Culmstock Bridge. It dates back to mediæval times with later repairs and alterations. Beside the bridge a gate leads you up onto the road opposite the Culm Valley Inn. Turn right to cross the bridge and walk back towards the war memorial from which you started.

Culmstock Bridge

Walk 10
Otterton & Ladram Bay
Distance: 7¾ miles / 12.5km

This fabulous route includes some astonishing coastline, attractive woodland and a 'quintessential Devon' village. It's reasonably easy underfoot and has only one steepish ascent but this is mostly under tree canopy and is a very pleasant stretch of the walk. The views are some of the best we know and there is plenty of opportunity for refreshment stops. Wild flowers abound during spring and summer – the cliffs turn pink with a haze of thrift. We had overseas visitors walking with us for this route and they were amazed by the scenery. Obviously, as with any coastal walk, there are edges near which you need to be cautious.

Map: OS Explorer 115, Exmouth & Sidmouth 1:25 000

Start point: Otterton Bridge. Post code: EX9 7HG. Grid ref: SY079852

Directions to start: Otterton lies 2½ miles north east of the coastal town of Budleigh Salterton. It is signed from the A3052

Parking: On-street parking in the village

Public Transport: The 157 operated by Stagecoach Devon passes through Otterton. Timetables available online at www.travelinesw.com. Nearest railway station is Exmouth (5.8 miles)

Distance: 7¾ miles

Refreshments: Coast Café and take away, Ladram Bay Holiday Park, 01395 568398; Kings Arms, Fore St, Otterton, 01395 568416; Otterton Mill, 01395 567041; Pebbles, Ladram Bay Holiday Park, 01395 568398

Toilets: At Otterton Mill for customers

Nearby places to stay: Kings Arms, Fore St, Otterton, 01395 568416; Otterton Mill, 01395 567041; The Old Post Office B&B, 17 Fore St, Otterton; Stoneborough House B&B, 21a East Budleigh Rd, Budleigh Salterton, 01395 445923

Nearby places of interest: A la Ronde (NT), Summer Lane, Exmouth, 01395 265514; Otterton Mill, Otterton, 01395 568521

Possible birds include: Blackbird, blue tit, buzzard, chiffchaff, cormorant, curlew, dunnock, fulmar, goldfinch, great tit, greenfinch, gulls of various hue, house martin, house sparrow, jackdaw, kestrel, kingfisher, linnet, little egret, magpie, mallard, moorhen, mute swan, oystercatcher, pheasant, raven, robin, rook, shag, shelduck, skylark, song thrush, stock dove, swallow, teal, wigeon, woodpigeon, wren – see also Authors' Tip

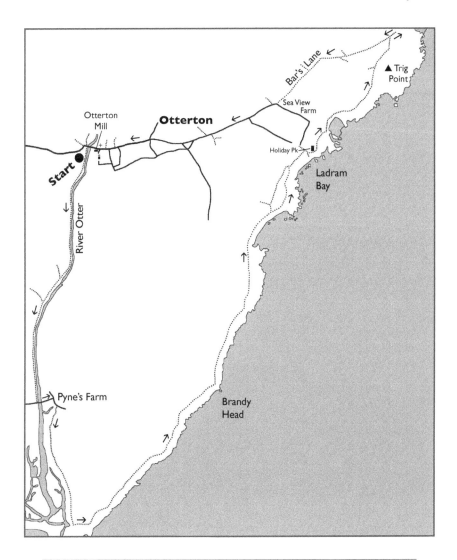

Authors' tip: Take binoculars and allow some time to sit in the hide. We have been lucky enough to see visiting rarities such as purple heron and glossy ibis, although we didn't see them on the day we did the walk for this book

---

The walk starts on the far side of the bridge from Otterton Mill. Take the footpath with the fingerpost directing you to Budleigh Salterton, 2¾ miles away along the river. There is a footpath leaving the bridge in the opposite direction so make sure you choose the correct one. Follow the clear path with the River Otter on your left, passing through a kissing gate by a footbridge about 400m from the village and continuing beside the river without crossing it. Pass through occasional gates and ignore any paths away from the river until you reach a tarmac road. This is 1½ miles from Otterton.

If you wish to visit Budleigh Salterton go straight on here as the path continues beside the river to the village. However, this is not part of the walk, which now continues left along the road for a short distance, crossing the river and walking towards Pynes Farm Shop. The road bends around and goes through the entrance gateway to the farm shop, South Farm and South Farm Court. By the gateway you will find a fingerpost directing you right along a footpath to the coast path, Ladram Bay and Sidmouth. Take this well-trodden path.

You are now walking with a field boundary to your right with some quite majestic trees. The path crosses a little wooden footbridge. Shortly beyond this keep a sharp lookout for a small path leading off right to a bird hide

Along the River Otter

Little egret photographed from bird hide

overlooking the estuary, a great place for bird watching.

When you've spotted all you can rejoin the path through the field towards the coast path. As you proceed you have a good view across the estuary towards Budleigh Salterton with the cliffs of the Jurassic Coast beyond. As you near the coast the path starts to bear left, keep going with it and soon good sea views open up showing the red Triassic sandstone of the cliffs along here. Eventually Ladram Bay with its massive rock stacks comes into view and, across the bay, nestling amongst the red cliffs, you can see the town of Sidmouth.

Continue on the coast path passing the ruined WWII Observation Point above Brandy Head – there is an interesting information board about it here. Ignore any paths inland and follow the coast towards Sidmouth. The stacks start to get much closer and the path begins to drop. You reach the rather surprising holiday park at Ladram Bay. Keep on the clifftop path below the caravans which are to your left – you are heading across a grassy area towards a building some way off within the complex. At the end of this grassy field bear left to a gate. Pass through and follow the path beyond towards an attractive thatched house. Keep following the coast path, as signed, past this house to reach Pebbles Restaurant and a pause for coffee and their excellent carrot cake if it's open.

Continue through the holiday park following the coast path and passing a play area. You are on a fenced path here. The stacks are now very close. Beyond the holiday park the path continues along the cliffs, beginning to climb towards High Peak. Spare a glance behind as you ascend – it's a beautiful view back along the coast.

As you continue uphill the path passes through the once-darkly-wooded area below High Peak. A broad path on the right leads up to the trig point

Ladram Bay and the Jurassic Coast

The Jurassic Coast, England's first natural World Heritage Site, totals some 95 miles of East Devon and Dorset coastline and is comprised of rock formations reflecting millions of years of the Earth's geological history, spanning the Triassic, Jurassic and Cretaceous periods. The oldest section of the  Jurassic Coast is in the west, at Exmouth, and the youngest in the east, at Studland Bay. The coastline around Ladram Bay is part of this World Heritage Site and the red sandstone stacks are the remnants of collapsed caves. The red colour is from iron oxide, and fossils found in the rocks indicate that their birthplace, over 200 million years ago, was a hot, desert region near the equator which from time to time had fertile river valleys flowing within it. Shifting land masses brought the rocks to their present location. The bases of the stacks are comprised of a more durable type of sandstone, resistant to sea erosion – hence the stacks are still standing.

Walking the Jurassic Coast

and information board about the 2012 archaeological dig; Stone Age and Dark Age (post-Roman) remains have all been found. It's a steep path up to the trig and the faint-hearted needn't take this there-and-back-again option.

The main path starts to descend and you emerge through a gate to find a three-way fingerpost sporting a small plaque which says High Peak East. Here the walk goes right for 100m before returning to this fingerpost. This short onward section is one of the gems of the route as you reach a bench with one of the loveliest views in England along the Jurassic Coast to Sidmouth (see photograph overleaf), where you can see Jacob's Ladder winding up the cliffs at the west end of the town. On a clear day you can see the Isle of Portland jutting out into the sea. Behind you from the bench are glorious inland views. Drink it in.

From here return 100m to the High Peak East post and continue along the track (Bar's Lane) with the woodland to your left and far-reaching country views beyond the boundary to your right. You are now heading back towards Otterton. Continue on the track beyond the woodland, ignoring any paths to right or left, until you reach Sea View Farm, 1km from the High Peak East fingerpost.

Another three-way fingerpost here directs you straight ahead along the lane for Otterton. Follow this, passing the entrance to the Ladram Bay Holiday Park on the left. Keep on the lane, ignoring any footpaths and enjoying glimpses of attractive houses, until you reach a staggered crossroads in the village. Keep straight ahead here along Fore Street, a very picturesque part of the village. This leads you back to your start point.

Spectacular view towards Jacob's Ladder and Sidmouth (Otterton walk)

Thatch abounds in glorious Otterton

Walk 11

Luppitt

Distance: 5¼ miles / 8.5km

This rather challenging walk in the Blackdown Hills has some superb views and passes through a very pretty village. At the time of our visit the Luppitt Inn was still owned and run by a lovely nonagenarian landlady whose family has owned the Inn for over 100 years. It maintains a very traditional atmosphere – the tiny bar is in her sitting room – and although no food is served the ale comes direct from the Otter Brewery just outside the village. (Long pipe!) The Inn is a delightful time capsule which needs to be treated with respect. Part of the route is on extremely boggy paths so this is not one to undertake if you wish to keep your boots clean. It is well way-marked and walkers are quite reliant on yellow arrows during some stretches. There are also some steep ascents – be prepared.

Map: OS Explorer 115, Exmouth & Sidmouth 1:25 000

Start point: Grid ref: ST180067. From the church in Luppitt the start point is 1.6 miles away. From here head south west down through the village and after 750m turn left. After another 700m turn left. Keep to the right as the road forks in 750m. The start point is then 350m on the right

Directions to start: The village of Luppitt lies 4 miles due north of Honiton. It can be accessed from both the A30 and A373 via country lanes

Parking: Some parking near farm gate (please don't block access) at start point

Public Transport: No buses in the village though the no 20, run by Stagecoach, calls in at nearby villages. Timetables available online at www.travelinesw.com. Nearest railway station is Honiton (3.9 miles)

Distance: 5¼ miles

Refreshments: Luppitt Inn (drinks only), 01404 891613; The Sidmouth Arms, Upottery, 01404 861252

Toilets: None en route

Nearby places to stay: Dolish Farmhouse B&B, Luppitt, 01404 891176; Lakeview Manor, Dunkeswell, 01404 891287

Nearby places of interest: Allhallows Museum of Lace, High St, Honiton, 01404 44966; Escot Park, Ottery St. Mary, 01404 822188

Possible birds include: Bullfinch, carrion crow, chaffinch, chiffchaff, goldfinch, house martin, jackdaw, pheasant, robin, swallow, willow warbler, woodpigeon, wren, yellowhammer

Authors' tip: Take a picnic – there's a convenient hidden bench just below the parking spot

Note: Be aware: part of this route is across high, open land, so the OS map and compass are useful – and clear weather conditions

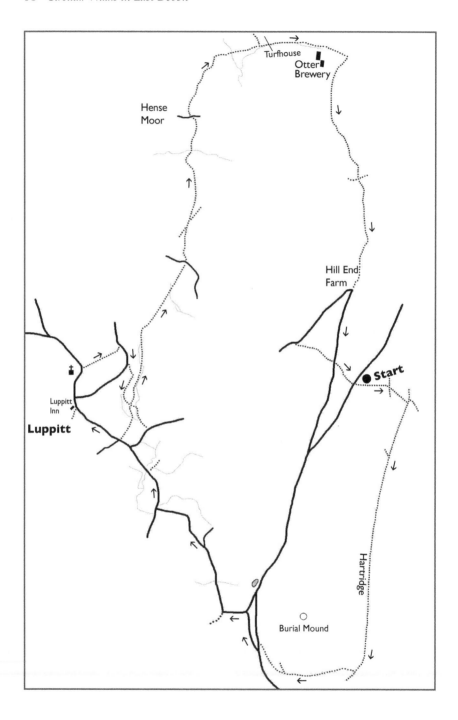

High up on Hartridge you will find a pull-in area near a farm gate where a clearly signed public footpath crosses the lane. There are massive views here across the top of Luppitt. Cross the stile next to the farm gate and head along the track away from the view, passing a corrugated iron 'barn' raised on oil drums! Far in the distance to the right you can see a very tall mast. The track bends right, passing through a boundary, and at the second right bend, 250m from the stile, you will see a yellow footpath arrow heading left. Ignore this and stay on the track as it heads south along Hartridge – the area of access land to the right of the track – you will also have glimpses of lovely, expansive views on the left.

Follow this track and after about 1km you will see the hedged enclosure of a tumulus on your right. Follow the track as it bends right, circumnavigating this ancient burial mound. Just after the bend the track forks. Keep right here, still walking beside the tumulus with the hedge to your right and good views to the left, including distinctive Dumpdon Hill. Pass through a farm gate and continue to a second gate. Beyond this take the left fork, heading downhill into the view. The track drops to a lane, turn left here for 30m then go right, downhill back on yourself.

Keep on the lane as it bends left towards houses and then goes right, passing Antelope Cottage on the left, followed by Shelves Farm. Follow the lane, ignoring any tracks to left or right, until you reach a T-junction. Go right here and walk through Luppitt, crossing the river and passing Dolish Farm on the left. Keep on the lane, you will find the Luppitt Inn also on the left and further along, and further uphill, St. Mary's Church. This is a lovely building dating back to about 1300 which is worth a visit. Notice the granite 'Millennium Bench' outside the porch and seek out the wooden bench under the magnificent yew with an inspiring view.

Opposite the main gate to the church is a clearly marked public footpath. Take this and walk through the field in the direction of its arrow heading down towards the bottom left corner and enjoying the views around you and back to the church. The gate leaving the field is just above the corner in the left hand hedge. Beyond this follow the path down to the metalled drive along which you turn right, this is a bridleway indicated by a blue arrow on a post. Within 50m, you will see another post with blue arrows,

Luppitt's fabulous setting in the Blackdown Hills

go left here along a track and this leads to a junction with a footpath in just over 200m.

Turn left along the footpath and follow this broad track which will lead you to Hense Moor. Beyond this point the walk starts to get boggy as you proceed and you will need to **keep a keen eye open** for the frequent yellow footpath arrows, which are a big help through this section. The route, which is sometimes indistinct, keeps in roughly the same direction for over 0.5km, through marshy bits, open areas and sometimes under trees until you reach a metalled drive, at which point you will find a stile up to the left, leading onto a drive.

Cross the drive and the stile opposite and after this bear left up through the trees. You enter an open field beyond the trees, keep going uphill for a short distance and then bear right to walk through the middle of the field along a broad, level area, away from the drive and at roughly 90° to it. There are lovely views down to the right here and you will also see a house up to the left.

Soon you reach a post bearing another yellow arrow, follow its direction to yet another arrow within about 200m. This one directs you right along a narrow path that almost immediately forks, keep right here, going slightly downhill. You will find another arrow in about 75m. The next yellow arrow, again roughly 75m from the last, points you right on the path, still dropping down to reach a footbridge.

Beyond the footbridge bear left, you are under trees through this area, and the path then bends right going uphill. Less than 200m from the footbridge the path rises to meet another metalled drive, there is a house down to your right here. Cross the drive and follow the arrowed path immediately opposite. This leads to a gate, continue beyond it on the narrow path and look out for the telegraph pole with a yellow arrow a short way from the gate. Go right at the fork beyond the pole and continue past two further telegraph poles with arrows – these arrows are very frequent and very necessary! After the third telegraph pole look for an ordinary post with an arrow that directs you right. The path drops down to a footbridge over a stream.

View to Dumpdon Hill

Dumpdon Hill

Dumpdon Hill is a distinctive Iron Age hill fort rising above the Otter Valley. The huge storm of 1990 uprooted many trees and exposed more of the history of the site which was in use about 2,500 years ago, although it was probably never a place of permanent habitation. Hill forts were our ancestors'  refuges, occupying high ground for ease of defence against would-be attackers. Such sites were usually surrounded by a stockade-type fence for protection but research indicates that Dumpdon may never have been fully completed. (see also feature on Sidbury walk.)

Beyond the bridge look for another yellow-arrowed telegraph pole about 30m away – you can still see the bridge from this point – and follow the arrow's direction through a very boggy bit. Pandora dog was up to her bottom in it. The path leads to a refreshingly open area in front of Turfhouse. From here follow the arrow that directs you right along their drive away from the house. Enjoy the ease of walking along the drive for nearly 400m. This is uphill but easy underfoot.

You meet a lane, go right here to enter the gates of Mathayes, home of the Otter Brewery. Walk through the parking area and as the drive goes right down to the brewery take the track going left uphill. You swiftly reach a footpath gate, go through here and walk beside the track – this is a recently re-routed stretch of footpath with more expansive views to the right. At the time of writing there was new construction occurring here but good provision had been made for the path. Head through the field following the direction of the top hedge with the field sloping away down to the right.

In the top corner of the field cross the stile and keep going through the next field in the same direction, with the boundary to your left and a fence to the right. As the right hand fence ends keep straight ahead, passing a tumbledown iron barn on the left, to a gate in the corner of the field with an arrow. Pass through and keep going, now with a fence to your left. Go through the next boundary where you will see the arrow directing you slightly right, going diagonally down the middle of the field to reach a gate in the opposite boundary.

Beyond here pass the stone outbuildings of idyllically-situated Hill End Farm, go through the entrance gate to join the lane at a hairpin bend. Keep ahead here, along the left hand lane, for 350m to a footpath on the left. Take this, dragging yourself uphill to pass a well-placed bench just below the lane and the point from which you started.

Enticing path

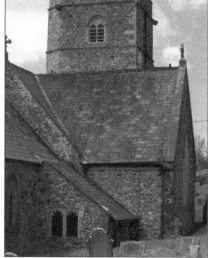

St Mary's Church

Walk 12

Membury

Distance: 3.3 miles / 5.3km

Step back in time on this delightful, short walk through historic countryside with glorious, pastoral views and the chance of roe deer. There are some climbs and occasional muddy patches but it's worth the effort!

Map: OS Explorer 116, Lyme Regis & Bridport 1:25 000
Start point: Outside village hall. Post code: EX13 7AF. Grid ref: ST276030
Directions to start: Membury village lies close to the border of Dorset and 3 miles north west of Axminster. It can be reached on lanes from either the A35, A30 or A358
Parking: Car park opposite village hall
Public Transport: No bus service. Nearest railway station is Axminster (3.2 miles)
Distance: 3.3 miles
Refreshments: See author's tip
Toilets: None en route
Nearby places to stay: Highfield B&B, Lyme Rd, Axminster, 01297 35714; Summer Lodge B&B, Dalwood, 01404 831470
Nearby places of interest: Burrow Farm Gardens, Dalwood, 01404 831285; Forde Abbey and Gardens, Chard, 01460 220231
Possible birds include: Blackbird, blue tit, buzzard, carrion crow, chiffchaff, coal tit, green woodpecker, house martin, house sparrow, jackdaw, jay, magpie, mallard, pied wagtail, swallow, wheatear, woodpigeon
Authors' tip: If you want a longer walk try linking this walk with Musbury. We did both on either side of lunch at The Golden Hind, Musbury

Turn left out of the car park and walk along the lane, passing the church of St. John Baptist and the war memorial on your right. Within 200m you reach a house called Membury Follie, turn left immediately after the house along their drive which is a public footpath. Beyond the house the path narrows. Follow it until it rises to meet a broader track along which you turn right.

You reach a remote cottage on the right and in another 30m you find a farm gate on the right with a yellow footpath arrow. Go through here and walk down the field keeping the boundary on your right for 150m, at

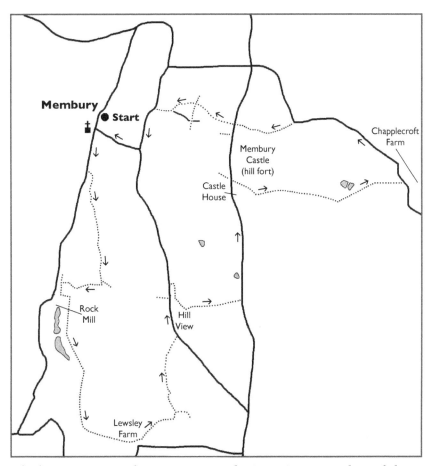

which point you reach a wide gap in the boundary. Pass through here, walking down the slope with houses over to the left. This leads to a yellow-arrowed gate, beyond which continue down beside the fence on the right to a big gate leading out of the field. Don't go through this gate but stay in the field and turn left to walk along the bottom of the field, keeping the boundary and the lane beyond it to your right and picking your way through the damp bits.

Keep ahead, with views across the beautiful, reflective ponds of Rock Mill down to your right. Follow the trodden path to the far side of the field and pass through the gate where a yellow arrow directs you through the next field, crossing a tiny, almost hidden bridge part-way across before rising to a gate in the far boundary. Here another yellow arrow points you obliquely left uphill through the next field to a stile and gate. Cross here and walk diagonally left through the middle of the next field to reach a footpath gate leading to a path between a cottage and its neighbouring barn.

Follow this path past the cottage (you're walking along its drive) and just before it bends right to reach the lane go left over a stile and puff up the field in the direction indicated by the fingerpost. This line brings you to another stile – don't cross it but turn left in the same field to follow the line of the top boundary keeping it to your right for almost 250m, there are lovely views to your left. Just before the end of the field you reach a yellow-arrowed gate on the right leading out of the field. Go through here and turn left along the track to the lane.

Turn left along the lane for 200m and after Hill View on the right take the footpath right off the lane. Enter the field and turn right, following the right hand boundary round for 350m to reach a gate leading onto another lane. Turn left and ascend with the lane for almost 500m until, less than

Church of St. John Baptist   *View of Rock Mill's gardens from the footpath*

View from Membury Castle

100m beyond Castle House on the right, you find another public footpath going right. Take this.

You are now climbing beside the right hand field boundary towards the hill fort of Membury Castle. Follow the right boundary with the rising ground of the fort to your left, crossing a stile (or passing beside it!) within 150m of entering the field. Keep going to reach a kissing gate, pass through and descend to another gate which enters a field. Follow the right hand boundary down the field to the bottom right hand corner and here another arrow directs you through a gate. Beyond this gate turn left to walk through the field keeping its boundary on your left.

When this boundary ends yellow-arrowed posts direct you through the rest of the field. You can see Chapplecroft Farm down to your right as you go. This line brings you to a lane along which you turn left. Follow this as it ascends and bends for about 550m to a T-junction. From here, keep straight ahead on the signed footpath to once more ascend the ramparts of Membury Castle – sorry!

Enjoy the views behind as you climb, but keep going up and very slightly left to reach a stile at the top under trees. Cross this and continue ahead, crossing the width of the hill fort and remembering those who once dwelt here. In about 50m, at the far side of the open area, an arrowed post directs you downhill beneath trees to a gate. Go downhill through the field towards a thatched cottage and a gate onto the lane.

Cross the lane and walk down the drive past the cottage to reach a further house on the right. Just beyond it, over to the left, a footpath gate leads into the field. Go through here, following the left boundary and ignoring options off, until, at the bottom, the field narrows under trees and brings you to a stile. Cross this and follow the track downhill to a drive. Turn right downhill and within 100m you reach the lane. Turn left, enjoying gateway views on the right back to the church, and in just over 150m turn right, heading down towards the village. You reach the church, turn right and you are back at your start point.

Membury

Archaeological digs around Membury show fragmented human occupation going back thousands of years BC, but the hill fort was occupied some 500 years BC and gives the village its name, which means 'strong fort' (see also feature on Sidbury walk). Roman artefacts have been found in the area and the earliest part of the church dates back to the 12thC. During the English Civil War there was at least one skirmish involving troops at Membury. Thomas Wakely, social reformer and founder of The Lancet, was born on a nearby farm in 1795. A bomb fell on the edge of the parish during WWII, killing two people, and Membury lost several other parishioners to the war. At the beginning of he 19thC there were 3 pubs in the village, now there is none. This idyllic village is far-removed from the M4 service station of the same name, which derives its name from a former WWII airfield.

Walk 13
Kentisbeare
Distance: 4.5 miles / 7.2km

This is a mostly level walk in the countryside surrounding a very pretty Devon village below the Blackdown Hills. It follows paths, tracks and some very quiet lanes. Depending on the time of year the hedgerows can be glorious with wild flowers. The inclines which you encounter during the latter part of the walk are reasonably gentle and you will be rewarded with good views towards the Blackdowns and the possible sighting of an elusive stoat. It can be muddy in places so wellies are advised in all but the driest of weather. Some of the stiles don't have any provision for dogs but Pandora – who is medium sized – negotiated all of them unaided. The village shop is a good place to stock up on chocolate and the lovely inn was, in recent years, saved from closure by becoming a community-run pub. It is now back in private ownership and is an extremely welcoming place to call in – it's also very dog friendly.

Map: OS Explorer 128, Taunton & the Blackdown Hills 1:25 000

Start point: Kentisbeare village centre. Post code: EX15 2AD Grid ref: ST068081

Directions to start: Kentisbeare is 4 miles east of Cullompton and signed off the A373 Cullompton to Honiton road

Parking: Park in the centre of the village – there is plenty of on-road parking

Public Transport: Bus operators that pass through Kentisbeare are: Dartline Coaches, Redwoods Travel, Stagecoach South West. Timetables available online at www.travelinesw.com. Nearest railway stations are Tiverton Parkway (3.9 miles) and Feniton (5.7 miles)

Distance: 4.5 miles

Refreshments: Post Office and Stores for en route snacks. Ashill Inn, Ashill, 01884 840506; Keepers Cottage, Nr Kentisbeare, 01884 266247; The Wyndham Arms, High St, Kentisbeare, 01884 266327

Toilets: None en route

Nearby places to stay: Orway Crescent Farm B&B, Orway, Kentisbeare, 01884 266876

Nearby places of interest: Coldharbour Mill, Uffculme, 01884 840960; Escot Park, Ottery St. Mary, 01404 822188

Possible birds include: Blackbird, blackcap, blue tit, buzzard, Canada goose, carrion crow, chaffinch, chiffchaff, collared dove, goldfinch, great spotted woodpecker, great tit, house martin, house sparrow, jay, magpie, mallard, mute

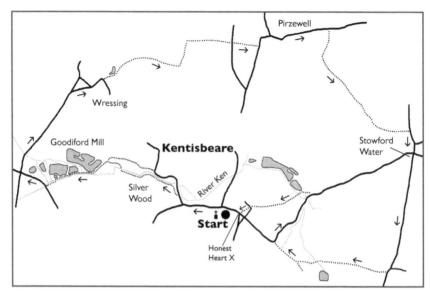

swan, pheasant, raven, robin, skylark, swallow, willow warbler, woodpigeon, wren

Authors' tip: If you're planning this walk on a Saturday you might also like to consider a haircut at the local pub! Dougie operates a gents' and boys' hairdressing service at the Wyndham Arms on Saturday mornings

Facing the Wyndham Arms turn right along the road passing the church on your left. This is Priest Hill and after a short distance becomes Silver Street. There are attractive houses along here and after a few hundred metres you pass a terrace of thatched cottages on your right, the last of these being Thatch Corner. Here take the lane on the right. In about 50m you find the entrance to the recently-planted Silver Wood on your left, one of the Woodland Trust's millennium community woodlands. Go through the small footpath gate into Silver Wood and follow the trodden path beyond. This young woodland has been planted with several open glades to create a lovely wildlife habitat.

About 50m from the gate the path passes a stone monument commemorating the planting of the wood. Beyond this the River Ken comes in to meet you on the right. Follow the path, crossing a small plank bridge, until you reach the footbridge spanning the river. Cross here and turn left at the end of the bridge, following the path to a stile less than 100m away. Negotiate this, leaving Silver Wood behind, and follow the narrow path beyond for about 50m to reach a more open area with a stile on the right. Ignore this stile and turn left to follow a broader path beside a fence, the ponds of Goodiford Mill Fishery over to your right.

Follow the path past the ponds and bear left to cross a footbridge. There are barns to your left here. Beyond the bridge cross straight over the track and go through the gate opposite which bears a footpath arrow. This enters an area of more ponds, walk through here keeping the fence and stream to your left. At the end of the ponds footpath arrows direct you left away from the fishing area then right through the car park. You see the house of Goodiford Mill ahead to your right. Beyond the car park is the lane. Turn right.

Within 200m you reach Goodiford Cross – here go right towards Wressing. Soon you reach a ford, which can be quite busy after rain but there is a convenient footbridge for the un-wellied. Keep going on the lane and just as you reach Wressing, immediately after Laurel House, take the right hand fork. There is a field to your right and a large, triangular paddock to your left. In 120m you reach another lane at a bend. Continue ahead here, slightly uphill along a windy road which passes Wressing Farm with its imposing gates on the right.

Just after this you find a stone barn on the left with a track leading ahead off the lane. Take this track, it goes gently uphill passing a pond over to the left, and follow it as it bends about until you reach a lane after ½ mile. Cross the lane and continue along the track opposite. There are lovely views ahead of you to the hills above Blackborough (explored in the Blackborough Walk). This short stretch of track drops to another lane along which you turn left. The lane then bends right, go with it, passing the houses of Pirzewell on the left and ignoring the left turn. (At this point

Between Wressing and Higher Pirzewell

it's worth mentioning that the spellings of Pirzewell and, later in the walk, Stowford vary greatly, in case you think we are getting it wrong!)

Pass the entrance to Pirzewell Ponds on your right and continue along the lane until you reach the house of Little Pirzewell with its striking monkey puzzle tree. Look for the stile on the right and cross here to enter a field. Walk straight ahead through the field with the hedge to your right, as directed by the footpath sign. A stream is running to your right with ponds beyond the boundary. This line leads to a stile. Cross it and continue beyond in the direction of the arrow on the stile, following the right hand boundary through two large fields and enjoying undulating views to your left until you reach a gate onto the lane.

Turn right along the lane to reach the tiny village of Stowford Water. At the T-junction bear right and in 50m at the next junction keep straight ahead towards Orway. You pass The White House with its red letter box on the right and the lane to the Baptist Church on the left. Keep going past Stowford Water Farmhouse and follow the lane with its expansive views for not quite ½ mile until you are joined by a lane from the left.

Almost back to Kentisbeare

St. Mary's Church, which in recent years has celebrated its 750th anniversary, is a fascinating building with many striking features. Although a Saxon church would have existed here no evidence of this remains. The present building was consecrated in 1259 and was much rebuilt in the 14th and 15th centuries, with later restoration. The rood screen dates back to around 1500 and the gallery was constructed during the reign of Charles I. Look carefully at the screen between the  chancel and the small chapel where fragments of the original colouring on the wood can still be seen. E. M. Delafield, author of 'Diary of a Provincial Lady' and one time president of Kentisbeare Women's Institute, is buried in the churchyard. Once you've explored, walk along the footpath that runs from the lychgate round the outside of the churchyard and from which you can get a rather remarkable view up into the branches of the ancient yew tree. If the church is locked visitors can obtain the key from the post office.

Keep ahead here and within about 20m you reach a track on the right. Follow this as it descends to enter a lightly wooded area. Keep along the broad track and beyond the trees you pass a house with associated outbuilding beyond which you reach a lane. Turn right.

Follow the lane for about 400m after which you reach a footpath signed to the left. Take this, going back on yourself away from the lane, through a pleasant leafy area until you reach a small footbridge and a stile with a footpath arrow. Cross the stile and walk diagonally right up the field in the direction of the arrow. This line leads to another stile. Pause here to enjoy views back down to the ponds behind you and across the valley towards Blackborough. A level path beyond the stile takes you through a field with a fence to the right and views down to the outskirts of Kentisbeare. At the end of the field cross the stile and go straight across the track to pick up a narrow footpath opposite. This leads beside a pretty cottage garden with free range chickens (watch your dogs!) to a stile followed by steps down to the lane. This junction has the delightful name of Honest Heart Cross. Turn right and follow the lane a short way back into Kentisbeare – a lovely end to a good walk.

Walk 14
Musbury
Distance: 3¾ miles / 6km

Huge, thirst-quenching views and wide open spaces are a feature of this walk, plus an Iron Age hill fort. Be prepared for some ascents but don't let them put you off, it's superb. The final stretch is a retrace with a glorious panorama.

Map: OS Explorer 116, Lyme Regis & Bridport 1:25 000	
Start point: Outside St. Michael's Church at the top of Church Hill. Post code: EX13 8BB. Grid ref: SY275945	
Directions to start: Musbury is situated on the A358 between the towns of Axminster and Seaton	
Parking: In car park below the church and next to the primary school. Post code: EX13 8BB	
Public Transport: The number 885 bus operated by Axe Valley Mini-Travel serves the village. Timetables available online at www.travelinesw.com. Nearest railway station is Axminster (2½ miles)	
Distance: 3¾ miles	
Refreshments: The Golden Hind, The Street, 01297 552413	
Toilets: None en route	
Nearby places to stay: Kate's Farm B&B, Lower Bruckland Farm, 01297 552861; Spillers Farm B&B, Seaton Rd (A358), 01297 551316	
Nearby places of interest: The Lyme Bay Winery, Shute, 01297 551355; Seaton Tramway, Colyton Station, Kingsdon, Colyton, 01297 20375; Shute Barton (NT), Shute, 01752 346585	
Possible birds include: Carrion crow, chaffinch, goldfinch, jackdaw, pheasant, robin, spotted flycatcher, swallow, wren	
Authors' tip: Don't leave this area before taking a trip on the Seaton Tramway. This lovely 3-mile route leaves Colyton to pass through the bird-rich Axe Valley en route to the seaside town of Seaton	

From the top of the lane near the church follow the signed footpath, which is the East Devon Way (EDW), leading into the beautiful gardens of Musbury Barton – this is a private house and gardens, please respect their privacy. Within 20m of the entrance, at the garages, go left on the drive, away from the house to reach the buildings of Musbury Farm. In the yard a clear footpath sign directs you right across a cattle grid and past the buildings. Follow the clear concrete track uphill away from the buildings. As the track levels out pause to admire the sweeping views back across the village.

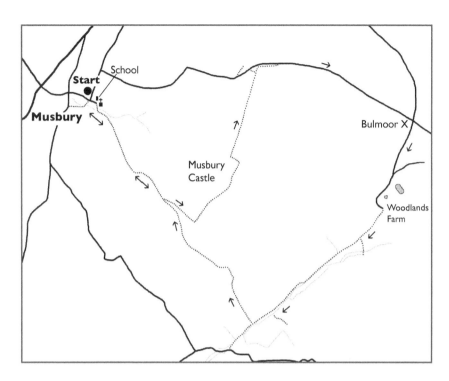

The track swings left and in less than 50m you find a public footpath going right. Take this, going uphill through the field as the finger directs, passing telegraph poles to your left and reaching a stile at the top of the field. Cross this and keep ascending as shown by the arrows on the stile. You reach a fingerpost on your left, keep ahead uphill – this is no longer the EDW – to reach the ridge at which point you have a glorious view towards Dorset. Turn left, you can still enjoy the view to the right, and you are now climbing gently beside the hill fort. Ignore any paths off (unless you wish to explore the top) skirting the fort and imagining the people who led their lives here centuries ago.

At the end of the open area you reach a stile with a yellow arrow. Cross it and continue ahead on a narrow path as indicated. Keep going until you reach a farm gate with a stile a few metres to its left, which was a bit overgrown at the time of writing. Cross it and turn left to another stile 40m away. Pause here for the view ahead, it is probably one of the more superbly-positioned stiles we know.

Cross the stile and turn right to follow the top boundary of the field, keeping the hedge to your right, view to your left. Keep on through the field to a stile at the end by a transmitter, then continue ahead – there are good views in front of you as well now. At the far end of the field ignore the stile to the left but cross the one in the top right hand corner, walking through the next field with the hedge on your left for 100m to reach the lane.

Turn right along the lane for 800m, on a sunny day this is an easy, 'dappled' stretch of walking and we saw no cars! At Bulmoor Cross turn right on a lane shown as 'no through road' – this is the EDW again – and descend, passing the entrance to Bulmoor House on the right. Ignore a left turn to Bulmoor Farm and keep straight ahead for about 100m, passing Woodlands Farm. The track turns left, go with it, downhill, and follow it as it bears right in less than 100m. When we passed there were some delightful, inquisitive pigs hereabouts!

Keep on down the track for 200m where you find a left bend and a footpath going ahead through a gate. Take the footpath, following the field hedge on your right. At the bottom keep ahead to leave the field on the obvious track. The heights of Musbury Castle are up to your right, hedge now to the left.

Musbury

There are several hill forts near the Devon-Dorset border and these were often occupied by tribes defending neighbouring territories from one another, the Dumnonii of Devon keeping a wary eye on the Durotridges of Dorset (see also feature on Sidbury Walk). It is thought that the hill fort of Musbury Castle,  although in present-day Devon, was used by the Dorset tribes. There is also evidence of Roman occupation and the village is mentioned in the Domesday Book of 1086. The oldest part of the current church is 15thC with later additions. Its striking Drake Monument was built in 1611 and extended a few decades later, the Drakes being a notable local family.

One of many beautiful views

Musbury and the countryside beyond

You reach a farmhouse on the right of the track, keep ahead along its tarmac drive. About 150m from the house look out for the three-way fingerpost directing you 90° right on a track, still, in effect, in the same field and now following a hedge to your left uphill towards the castle. After a stile continue to climb, going ahead then left along the line of the hedge. Up at the next fingerpost you are directed left into the trees – you will see a big metal tank over to the left in the woodland. Keep going up on the path to emerge into a field. Here a yellow arrow on a post points you up to the top left corner of the field where you will find a gate.

Go through this gate and a fingerpost beyond displays a yellow arrow pointing you up to a metal gate. Beyond the gate keep going up and at the top of the bank an arrow points you ahead towards trees – enjoy the view left here. Once in the trees follow the clear path then pass through a gate and head up to a fingerpost which you may remember!

Here turn left, you are now retracing your steps down to a stile. Cross this and walk diagonally right down the field you ascended earlier – forgive us this retrace but we feel it's a superb way to finish the walk! The views across the expanse of the Axe Valley are wonderful and to the left is the sea at Seaton. You reach the stile onto the track, turn left along it and descend once more to Musbury Farm. Turn left out of their yard, along the drive of Musbury Barton and back to the church.

Walk 15
Sidbury & Sidford
Distance: 8½ miles / 13.7km

This walk, although rather longer than others in this book, provides for a great day out with plenty of refreshment stops and lots of variety. It is a walk of glorious viewpoints, some of them vast, some chocolate-boxy, which make the climbs worth the effort. You'll find magnificent trees along lovely woodland and field paths. At one point you cross a nature reserve where you might be lucky enough to spot the rare Dartford Warbler and nightjars – one of the authors has been here in the evening and heard the latter. The walk also encompasses two historic villages with some pretty cottages.

Map: OS Explorer 115, Exmouth & Sidmouth 1:25 000

Start point: Outside St. Giles' Church. Post code: EX10 0SD. Grid ref: SY139917

Directions to start: Sidbury is located on the A375 approximately 6½ miles south west of Honiton

Parking: Free car park on Ridgeway Close. Post code: EX10 0SN

Public Transport: The 52B and 56B Stagecoach Devon buses stop at Sidbury. Timetables available online at www.travelinesw.com. Nearest railway stations are Feniton (5.6 miles) and Honiton (5.8 miles)

Distance: 8½ miles

Refreshments: Blue Ball Inn, Steven's Cross, Sidford, 01395 514062; Red Lion Inn, Fore St, Sidbury, 01395 597 313; Rising Sun, School St, Sidford, 01395 513722; Sidmouth Garden Centre Restaurant, Stowford, 01395 516142

Toilets: Behind village hall in Sidbury and in centre of Sidford

Nearby places to stay: Blue Ball Inn, Steven's Cross, Sidford, 01395 514062; Rose Cottage, Greenhead, Sidbury, 01395 597357

Nearby places of interest: Beer Quarry Caves, Quarry Lane, Beer, 01297 680282; The Donkey Sanctuary, Sidmouth, 01395 578222

Possible birds include: Blackbird, carrion crow, goldfinch, green woodpecker, gulls of various hue, house martin, jackdaw, linnet, long-tailed tit, magpie, raven, robin, swallow, woodpigeon, wren

Authors' tip: Although slightly off route we would highly recommend a detour to the Rising Sun in Sidford which does excellent food

---

With the church to your left and the Red Lion Inn to your right walk away from the centre of the village passing the splendid Court House on the

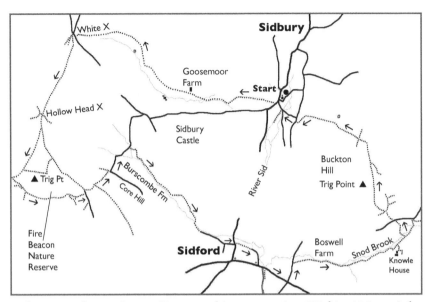

right – watch out for traffic near this start point. Within 100m of the church, just at the end of the wall of Court House, you find a footpath fingerpost pointing you right to White Cross along a stony track. Take this. The rough track becomes tarmac, passing houses, and as the tarmac ends keep straight ahead along a track, there is a yellow footpath arrow along here plus a pink East Devon Way (EDW) arrow – and this is your direction. Look out for the EDW's foxglove symbol on the posts.

You reach a farm gate, keep going past a barn on the left to enter a field. Continue, following the right hand hedge. The hill ahead and to your left is the hill fort of Sidbury Castle. Enjoy the views behind as you ascend this field and at the top go right through the gate, still following the pink arrows. This narrow stretch of field broadens out, keep going to reach a metal gate beyond which is a tarmac farm drive. Turn right along it, crossing a stream to reach the buildings of Goosemoor Farm. Pass the house on your right and keep straight ahead through a gate to join a path, still walking in the same direction and going uphill.

It is a long stretch up this track and you eventually rise to meet a gate with arrows on the left post. Follow their direction through the field beyond. At the far side of this field pass through the boundary, walking up the next field towards trees – you can see a yellow-topped post high up near the trees to help guide you. When you reach the post pause – to draw breath and to admire the sea view behind.

From the post follow the arrow's direction towards the treed boundary and pass through it to follow more arrows which point you ahead, along another line of trees and keeping the fence over to your right. Follow this direction, beside the fence to your right and passing through another boundary to eventually reach a footpath gate with the usual signs. Keep ahead beyond this through the next field, now with the boundary on your left. When this ends keep straight on across the field where you will find a gate onto a track. This leads to a lane, turn right along it.

This is White Cross. You swiftly reach an area of car park with immense views. Savour them then seek out the track at the end of the parking area furthest from the lane – not the footpath at the edge of the view. Follow the track under trees and within 100m you find signs saying 'no vehicular access apart from agricultural access'. Keep ahead between these. This is still the EDW and a lovely stretch of verdant woodland walking.

The lofty heights of White Cross

Fire Beacon Plantation

When you emerge from the woodland keep ahead on the track for another 500m or so to where you will find a meeting of ways at Hollow Head Cross. Keep straight ahead on the pink arrowed EDW, also denoted as 'Coleridge Link' – Samuel Taylor Coleridge having been born in nearby Ottery St. Mary. In approximately 120m you reach a point at which a 'County Road' forks left but you keep ahead on the EDW which at this point also becomes a bridleway – you are basically continuing in the same direction as before, don't be tempted by any other forestry tracks which deviate off. You are walking through Fire Beacon Plantation and there is a superb ancient boundary of trees on your left.

At the end of the wood you reach a metal gate and the EDW continues across Fire Beacon Nature Reserve. Keep ahead here on the left fork, still the bridleway – ignore the right fork. You are walking with expansive views towards the sea and 300m away you may be able to spot a fingerpost. When you reach it, greet it but ignore its left turn and keep straight on. At the right time of year the gorse and heather through this stretch is very colourful.

Keep ahead at the next fingerpost, within 100m. The path descends and you can see Sidmouth to your left, nestling in its valley. Arrows keep you in the right direction until, about 150m from the fingerpost which you greeted but ignored, the EDW takes a sharp left turn. At this point look out for the wonderful age-smoothed root system of the tree opposite. Keep going downhill to reach another nature reserve board by a meeting of ways. About 10m beyond the board a yellow arrowed footpath goes left and this is what you follow, now leaving the bridleway and EDW which go right at this point.

Follow the footpath and within about 150m there is a rather indistinct fork at which you need to keep left up two steps – at the time of writing a leaning yellow arrow helped direct you. Keep on this well-arrowed path, enjoying the curved bench which you come across along the way. This has another lovely view over Sidmouth. Crack open the apple juice then keep on along the clear path which can be a bit damp but some boardwalk helps. Beyond the boardwalk the path winds past a wonderful, horizontal tree which fell out of the bank years ago but continues to grow – a real survivor.

About 150m beyond this tree you may spot a footpath going right, but ignore it anyway and follow the ongoing path to reach a footbridge with

Sidbury Castle

The Iron Age hill fort of Sidbury Castle is about 185m above sea level. Such forts were constructed by our ancestors on naturally-occurring high ground in order to provide somewhere to live and trade which might be reasonably easy to defend by virtue of its height. Some theories also suggest that hill  forts were enlarged and enhanced as a display of power by tribal chiefs. Sidbury's fort was protected by a rampart and ditch surrounding the top of the hill. There is evidence of much later, post-mediæval earthworks on Sidbury. In the 19thC a hoard of sling stones was found here. These are now in Exeter Museum. There is no public right of way onto the castle.

a stile beyond it. Cross the field after this to another stile leading onto the lane. Turn left for 50m along the lane to reach a footpath going right into Core Hill Wood. Take this and keep ahead in the wood (don't fork left as you enter it) and follow what becomes a sunken track under trees.

Within 200m of entering this wood the path opens into a meeting of ways and up to your right you will see a wooden post with yellow arrows. Climb up to this, and from it keep straight ahead – you are walking towards the buildings of Burscombe Farm which you can see in the distance through the trees. The path drops down in the direction of the farm and in about 100m reaches a metal gate on the left. Pass through and turn right to keep the boundary and trees on your right. The boundary ends but keep straight down the field to reach a stile, the heights of Sidbury Castle beckon across the valley.

The stile, when you get there, is at a bit of a wild angle but is more secure than you first think! Cross it and go down to the lane, where you are met by three options. Take the middle lane, still heading down towards Burscombe Farm. When you reach the farm, just before the house, look for a footpath going right off the lane. Take this and follow the track away from the gate as shown by the fingerpost. The house and garden are to your left. The track bends slightly right, keep going to the far side of the field where you will find a gate. Go through this and keep ahead through the next field, which slopes up to your left with the boundary to your right. Part-way through this field you will see an arrow on a post pointing obliquely right onto a sunken path below the field. Follow this beside a stream and keep going as the yellow arrows direct to eventually emerge at the end of the same field with a track ahead of you.

Follow this track (still in the same direction as before) for 200m, at which point look out for a fingerpost directing you left. Take this, climbing up into a field then keeping ahead with the boundary to your right. Keep ascending through the field and you will see the outskirts of Sidford ahead. Follow the right hand boundary as it descends, with Brook Farm down to your right, and stay beside the right hand boundary through the fields until it bends right to meet a stile by a fingerpost leading onto the tarmac farm drive.

Go left along the drive to reach the houses of Sidford. Keep ahead along this residential road until you meet one of the main roads into Sidford. From here the walk crosses the road and turns left for 20m to a narrow path going right. Take this. (NB. If you are going to The Rising Sun go right along the main road to where you will find the inn and the crossroads. Come back to the narrow path after lunch.)

This little path emerges at a cream-coloured house, Mill House. Keep ahead and bend right with the lane, passing Ballard Grove to eventually reach St. Peter's Church. Turn left along the road, keeping to the pavements and crossing the 12thC packhorse bridge, a scheduled ancient monument, over the River Sid. Keep on the main road for almost 400m until you reach the crossroads at the end of the village, then go left along Harcombe Lane East.

Keep on the lane for 200m to reach the drive to Boswell Farm on the right. This is a public bridleway (although at the time of writing there was no sign), follow it, the Snod Brook babbling away beside you, and pass the entrances to Boswell Cottages and the farmhouse. This is a pleasant, easy stretch of walking. Keep on the drive beyond a cattle grid, you are heading for Knowle House through some lovely countryside. You reach some large stone gateposts at another cattle grid 1.1km (0.7 miles) after first joining this drive. Keep along the drive as it bends right to reach the main entrance gates to Knowle House, now a care home.

Here you will find a fingerpost indicating a sharp left turning along a bridleway. Take this, passing a cottage on your left. In 50m keep ahead through a bridleway gate and after a further 100m reach a second gate and go left on the yellow-arrowed footpath. It can be rather mucky through here, pick your way down to the footbridge over the Snod. Post-Snod keep ahead with the field boundary to the left, then veer right to pass in front of Harcombe Farmhouse. At the end of the house go left to leave the field along the track between the house and barns.

You reach a lane, turn left for 20m to an unmetalled road leading right off the lane. Take this and follow it uphill for just over 100m to a fork. Go left on the footpath and in about 20m cross the stile on the right. Beyond here walk up beside the left hand boundary of the field towards the trees of Buckton Hill. Pause occasionally as you climb to admire the pastoral scene behind you.

At the top of the field a stile leads onto a narrow path – keep going up it. Look out for the beautiful, blue-bellied dor beetles on this path and don't step on them – they have an important job to do: eating their own weight in dung every day they are nature's countryside cleansing operatives. Puff up this path, enjoying views to the right, for 600m, after which you'll find a yellow-arrowed post as a path comes up from the right. Keep ahead here and within another 100m another yellow-arrowed post points you diagonally left up some steps and deeper into the woodland, still climbing. You reach a stile near a sign which tells you that you're just leaving Buddle Wood. Beyond the stile go straight ahead across a small field to emerge on a crossing bridleway.

Go right and within 20m go left at the three-way fingerpost – this is once more the East Devon Way. Follow the path going under the trees and in just over 100m you meet an old bank boundary ahead. Go right and swiftly left again, as shown by arrows, to basically keep on in the same direction. The path now drops steeply down through the trees – get your knees in gear and mind how you go! At the bottom of the wood you land on a plank bridge.

Negotiate the fence at the end of the bridge – the top bar lifts to allow a more elegant arrival in the field than one of the authors managed, getting herself stuck astride the fence before realising it was hinged for ease of climbing. The trickiness of the descent through the woodland is now rewarded with the walk across the field into a glorious view of Sidbury – head across aiming slightly left of the church tower.

At the bottom of the field leave via the stile and follow the pink arrow, keeping the boundary to your right. This brings you to a gate beyond which bear left through the field as directed, passing Long Barn House down to the right – notice its beautiful clock. At the end of an open barn go right to a kissing gate leading onto the lane. Turn right along the lane and within 30m go left to drop down into Sidbury, crossing the bridge and passing some idyllic cottages to reach the main road near the church from which you started. A lovely end to a good walk.

Returning to Sidbury

Thatched forge (NT), Branscombe (Walk 1)

View near Musbury Castle (Walk 14)

Ladram Bay on the Jurassic Coast (Walk 10)

Bejewelled cobwebs (Walk 15)

All images used in this book are available as cards and prints from Culm Valley Publishing
www.culmvalleypublishing.co.uk

Other guides by the same authors

Circular Walks in Central Devon
ISBN: 978-1-907942-01-3
£6.99
Fifteen walks through the hidden countryside of Mid Devon

A Dozen Dramatic Walks in Devon
ISBN: 978-1-907942-00-6
£5.99

A Dozen Dramatic Walks in Cornwall
ISBN: 978-1-907942-03-7
£5.99

A Dozen Dramatic Walks in Somerset
ISBN: 978-1-907942-02-0
£5.99

A Dozen Dramatic Walks in Dorset
ISBN: 978-1-907942-04-4
£5.99
The Dozen Dramatic series takes you to the most spectacular scenery each county has to offer. All walks are circular.

Town Walks in Devon
ISBN: 978-1-907942-05-1
£7.99

Town Walks in Cornwall
ISBN: 978-1-907942-06-8
£6.99
Shortish, circular walks exploring the history (and tea shops!) of Devon and Cornwall's fascinating towns.

All books available from Culm Valley Publishing: 01884 849085
www.culmvalleypublishing.co.uk / info@culmvalleypublishing.co.uk